SERIAL KILLERS

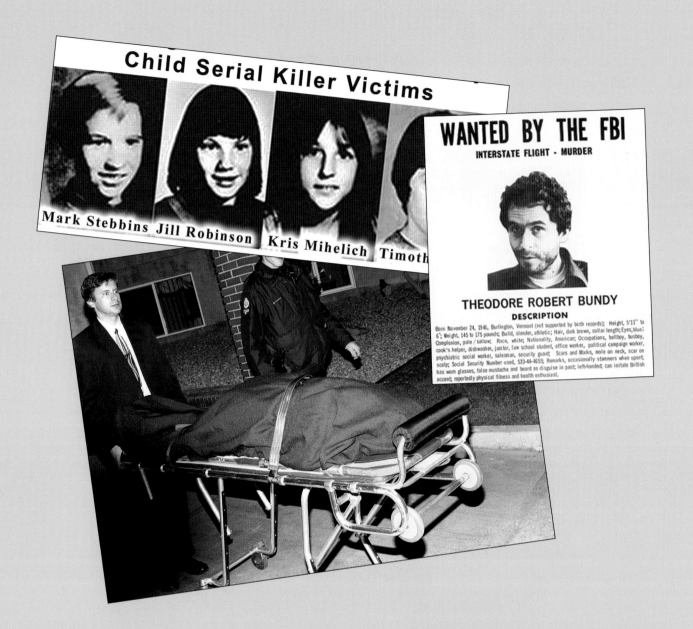

DRUG CARTELS AND SMUGGLERS
INFAMOUS TERRORISTS
MASS MURDERERS
MODERN-DAY PIRATES
ORGANIZED CRIME
SERIAL KILLERS

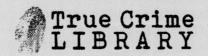
True Crime
LIBRARY

SERIAL KILLERS

SETH H. PULDITOR

ELDORADO INK

Eldorado Ink
PO Box 100097
Pittsburgh, PA 15233
www.eldoradoink.com

Produced by OTTN Publishing, Stockton, New Jersey

CPSIA compliance information: Batch#CS2013-6. For further information,
contact Eldorado Ink at info@eldoradoink.com.

First printing

1 3 5 7 9 8 6 4 2

Library of Congress Cataloging-in-Publication Data
available from the Library of Congress

ISBN-13: 978-1-61900-043-8 (hc)
ISBN-13: 978-1-61900-044-5 (trade)
ISBN-13: 978-1-61900-045-2 (ebook)

*For information about custom editions, special sales, or premiums,
please contact our special sales department at info@eldoradoink.com.*

TABLE OF CONTENTS

SERIAL MURDER: AN INTRODUCTION 7

DAVID BERKOWITZ: THE "SON OF SAM": 16

TED BUNDY: CHARISMATIC KILLER 24

ANGELO BUONO JR. AND KENNETH BIANCHI: HILLSIDE STRANGLERS 36

EDWARD GEIN: SHY PSYCHO 42

JACK THE RIPPER 45

HERMAN W. MUDGETT: DR. H. H. HOLMES 53

DENNIS RADER: THE BTK KILLER 58

GARY RIDGWAY: THE GREEN RIVER KILLER 64

HAROLD SHIPMAN: DEADLY DOCTOR 74

FRED WEST: THE MONSTER OF GLOUCESTER 80

AILEEN WUORNOS: VICTIM TURNED KILLER? 85

CHAPTER NOTES 88

GLOSSARY 90

FURTHER READING 91

INTERNET RESOURCES 92

INDEX / PICTURE CREDITS 93

SERIAL MURDER
AN INTRODUCTION

Serial killers have a powerful hold on the public imagination. "It's not just the gruesomeness of what they do," notes Dr. Harold Schechter, an expert on the subject, "it's that the lives they lead have some kind of symbolic meaning for us. The serial killer has become this mythic figure. . . . It is clear that the serial killer has become the incarnation of all of our dreads and anxieties."

It's not difficult to understand why. Many serial murderers find satisfaction in the very act of killing. Often their lives are a perpetual cycle of fantasizing about murder and finding victims on whom to enact their murderous fantasies. The idea that we might unknowingly cross paths with, and be targeted by, such a person is a terrifying prospect indeed.

It is also, statistically, a very unlikely prospect. The Federal Bureau of Investigation estimates that serial killers commit less than 1 percent of all homicides in the United States. Extrapolating from the total number of homicides recorded in recent years, we might expect serial killers to be responsible for about 120 to 180 murders in the United States annually. In a nation of more than 300 million people, the odds of falling victim to a serial murderer are thus exceedingly small. That, of course, does not minimize the terrible suffering of victims and their families, or suggest that catching serial murderers is not a significant problem for law enforcement.

Many people assume that serial murder is a recent phenomenon. It isn't. Two serial killers spotlighted in this volume—Jack the Ripper and Herman Mudgett—were active in the late 19th century. And there is substantial evidence of serial killers from much earlier still. For example, the French nobleman Gilles de Rais (1404–1440) confessed to sexually abusing, torturing, and murdering more than 140 children. Before his capture in 1589, a farmer named Peter Stumpp is believed to have murdered and eaten at least 16 people in the Electorate of Cologne (present-day Germany). Erzsébet Báthory (1560–1614), a Hungarian countess, tortured and killed girls and young women. Her victims may have numbered in the hundreds, and she is said to have bathed in their blood.

Gilles de Rais

Contemporaries of Gilles de Rais, Stumpp, and Báthory had no rational explanation for such shocking behavior. Instead, they attributed particularly gruesome murders to the influence of supernatural forces (for example, demons or the devil) or to fanciful conditions like lycanthropy (the transformation of a person into a wolf).

During the 1800s, practitioners of the emerging disciplines of criminology, psychology, and psychiatry first sought to explain the behavior of violent criminals in scientific terms. Some of the theories put forward have since been debunked. For example, the Italian physician and criminologist Cesare Lombroso (1835–1909) asserted that some people inherited a tendency toward criminality as a vestige of humanity's savage past. These "born criminals," Lombroso said, were identifiable by certain physical characteristics, such as unusually long arms, a protruding jaw, and a sloping forehead. By contrast, the German psychiatrist Richard von Krafft-Ebing (1840–1902)

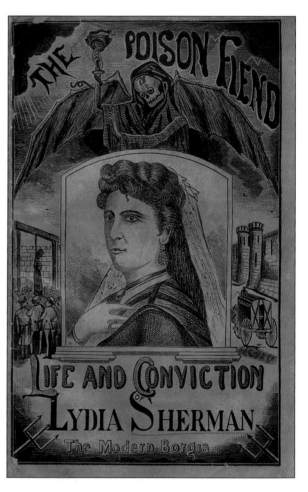

American serial murderer Lydia Sherman poisoned three husbands with arsenic to collect insurance payouts, and also killed seven of her children. She was convicted in 1872 and sentenced to life in prison.

had insights that have stood the test of time. Krafft-Ebing noted a connection between sexual lust and a desire to kill in some murderers. He also proposed that for these "lust killers," acts like the postmortem mutilation of a victim might function as a substitute for sex.

For the first seven decades of the 20th century, however, few people had even heard the term *lust killer*, much less understood the psychology of these offenders. This was true not only among the general public but also within law enforcement circles. On occasion, a string of sexually based homicides attracted massive publicity. In one of the most notorious of these cases, that of the Boston Strangler, a handyman named Albert DeSalvo confessed to sexually assaulting and murdering 11 women between 1962 and 1964. But such cases, which occurred only rarely, were referred to as "mass murders"— the same designation given to cases in which a killer claimed multiple lives in a single incident (usually with a firearm).

Robert K. Ressler, a special agent at the FBI's Behavioral Science Unit, was among those who recognized that killing many people at one time and killing many people individually over a longer period were distinct offenses. In the 1970s, Ressler coined the term *serial murder* to describe the latter. *Mass murder* remained the preferred term for the former.

The United States witnessed a spate of highly publicized serial murder cases during the 1970s and early 1980s. In 1971 a Mexican-American labor contractor named Juan Corona was convicted of murdering 25 migrant farmworkers in northern California. John Wayne Gacy tortured, sexually assaulted, and murdered at least 33 teenaged boys and young men between 1972 and 1978. Gacy—a successful building contractor, amateur clown, and minor figure in Chicago politics—buried most of his victims in the crawl space beneath his house. Ted Bundy left victims across at least seven states. A onetime law

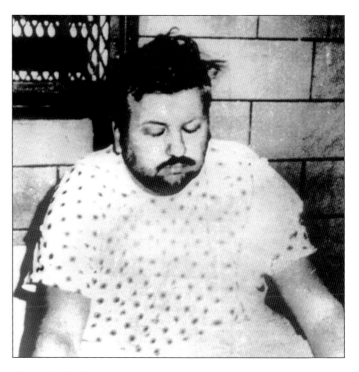

Serial killer John Wayne Gacy in prison, circa 1978. Between 1972 and 1978 Gacy murdered at least 33 boys and young men, burying many of his victims under his home.

Richard Ramirez, nicknamed "the Night Stalker," was a Satanist who killed more than a dozen people in California during 1984 and 1985. Convicted of numerous rapes and murders, he remains on California's death row awaiting execution.

student, Bundy confessed to murdering 30 young women from 1974 to 1978, but his actual death toll might have been considerably higher. A serial killer preying on African-American boys and youths terrorized Atlanta between 1979 and 1981. Photographer Wayne Williams was convicted of two homicides, and Atlanta police attributed an additional 22 killings to him.

These cases, as well as other widely reported ones that occurred during the same period, led many ordinary Americans to the terrifying if erroneous conclusion that a new type of homicidal predator was emerging. Criminologists, meanwhile, recognized the critical need for a better understanding of serial murder.

Pioneering research was conducted in the late 1970s under the leadership of Robert Ressler. Ressler and fellow FBI behavioral profilers such as John Douglas interviewed at length 36 incarcerated murderers, of whom 25 were serial killers. Most of the serial killers reported suffering physical, sexual, or emotional abuse during childhood, often at the hands of parents. Most had displayed, during childhood or adolescence, at least one of the three behaviors that make up the so-called Macdonald triad: enuresis, or bedwetting, well past school age; the starting of fires; and the torturing of animals. Without exception, the serial killers reported having vivid, violent fantasies, which they eventually sought to act out with real human victims. Ressler and his colleagues concluded that serial murder almost always involves sexual motivations, whether or not there is any overt sexual contact between the offender and victims. They also asserted that only men commit serial murder.

From their interviews with offenders and the close examination of cases, Ressler and his colleagues divided serial killers into two broad categories: "organized" and "disorganized." Organized serial killers are of higher intelligence. Socially adept, they may be married or living with a partner. They tend to use charm, verbal persuasion, or some kind of ruse to gain the trust of potential victims. They usually target strangers. Organized killers plan their crimes meticulously and control their emotions during the commission of those crimes. Geographically mobile, they often move their victims' bodies to a different location from where the vic-

In the late 1970s and early 1980s, FBI agents John Roberts (left) and Robert Ressler helped develop techniques for identifying, capturing, and interrogating serial killers through behavioral profiling.

tims were murdered. Organized killers follow the media response to their murders closely. They also follow the police investigations, and they enjoy communicating with police and may volunteer information.

Disorganized offenders, by contrast, tend to be of average or slightly below average intelligence. If they are employed, it is usually in a low-skill job. Socially awkward, disorganized killers typically live alone, don't have a steady romantic partner, and rarely if ever date. They rely on sudden, "blitz-style" attacks to incapacitate victims. During the commission of their crimes, they experience a great deal of emotional unrest, and after a murder they will display major behavioral or personality changes. They sometimes show up at the funeral of a victim. They usually live or work near the scene of their murders, and they don't typically move victims' bodies away from crime scenes.

From careful analysis of a crime scene, Ressler and his colleagues believed, it's possible to determine whether a killer is organized or disorganized. And from that information, a profile of the likely offender can begin to be assembled, enabling the police to focus their investigation. Of course, the organized/disorganized dichotomy is just the beginning of a criminal profile; more specific information can often be gleaned from a crime scene.

In the *Crime Classification Manual*, John Douglas, Robert Ressler, and colleagues delineated serial murder as "three or more separate events in three or more separate locations with an emotional cooling-off period between homicides." Further, they said,

> The serial murder is hypothesized to be premeditated, involving offense-related fantasy and detailed planning. When the time is right for him and he has cooled off from his last homicide, the serial killer selects his next victim and proceeds with his plan. The cooling-off period can last for days, weeks, or months and is the key feature that distinguishes the serial killer from other multiple killers.

This definition of serial murder remains widely accepted, though many

During the fall of 2002, John Allen Muhammad (above, left) and Lee Boyd Malvo (above, center) terrorized the Washington, D.C., area with a series of sniper attacks that killed 10 people. The duo modified their car, drilling a hole in the trunk (top right) so that they could shoot their victims without being seen. (Bottom right) A rifle used in the killings is pictured on the car seat. The "DC Snipers" were caught on October 24, 2002. Muhammad was executed in 2009. Malvo, who was only 17 at the time of the murders, is currently serving multiple life sentences.

others have been offered over the years, and the FBI recently reduced to two the required number of homicides in its definition of serial murder.

In other respects, subsequent studies have also borne out much of the original FBI research, at least in its general outlines. Childhood abuse and abandonment are, in fact, strongly linked to serial murder later in life (though only a very small minority of people who suffer such abuse go on to become serial killers). Many, but not all, serial killers have a history of setting fires and torturing animals, though researchers are increasingly skeptical of a connection between enuresis and serial murder. Many, but not all, captured serial killers report being driven by violent fantasies.

On the other hand, Ressler and his colleagues were clearly wrong in stating that all serial killers are male. Women, it is now almost universally conceded, make up a small but significant proportion of serial killers (estimates range up to about 15 percent). This book profiles one such murderer, Aileen Wuornos. The early FBI profilers also erred in assuming that serial murder invariably has sexual aspects. In recent years, for example, dozens of cases have been uncovered of health care providers committing serial murder through lethal drug injections or by tampering with medical equipment. Some of these killers see themselves as angels of mercy, ending the suffering of ill patients. Others—like the notorious British doctor Harold Shipman, whose case is examined in this book—may simply be fascinated by their power over life and death, or may enjoy watching people die. But they aren't motivated by sex.

Various experts have sought to categorize the full spectrum of serial murderers. One of the more popular typologies was put forward in 1988 by Ronald M. Holmes, a coroner and criminal

While working in a California medical center during the 1990s, Efren Saldivar killed at least six people, and possibly dozens more, by injecting them with lethal doses of drugs. He was convicted in 2002 and sentenced to six consecutive life terms.

justice professor, and James E. DeBurger, a sociologist. Holmes and DeBurger identified four essential types of serial killers:

1. Visionary—These offenders act in response to hallucinatory voices, visions, or other delusions they believe command, compel, or guide them to kill.

2. Mission-Oriented—These killers believe their task is to rid society of certain classes of undesirable people, such as prostitutes or members of a specific racial or ethnic group.

3. Hedonistic. These killers gain satisfaction or pleasure either from the act of murdering or from the results of murders. Included in the former group would be lust killers and "thrill killers" (who murder for excitement). Included in the latter would be killers who murder to attain what they regard as a better lifestyle (for example, a woman who murders a succession of husbands for their money).

4. Power/Control-Oriented. These killers find emotional fulfillment in exercising complete power over their victims. Many especially enjoy watching their terrified victims plead for mercy.

Some experts question the value of Holmes and DeBurger's typology, as well as all other efforts to classify serial killers by outlook or motivation. Such critics frequently point out that a serial murderer's motivations may be mixed—many lust killers, for instance, also find pleasure in completely dominating and controlling their victims. Also, a killer's motivations may shift over time. Moreover, the actual reasons for murdering may never be apparent to anyone but the killer himself. Each serial killer, like every other person, is unique. So trying to classify killers, critics say, isn't the best use of investigatory resources.

One thing all experts in the field agree on is that—contrary to the assumptions of many nonspecialists—only a small minority of serial killers are insane. It is estimated that just 2 percent to 4 percent of serial killers are afflicted by psychosis, a loss of contact with reality that is typically characterized by disordered thought patterns, delusions, and visual or auditory hallucinations. Examples of psychotic serial killers (classified as "visionary" under the Holmes and DeBurger typology) include Richard Trenton Chase and Herbert Mullin. Both men suffered from paranoid schizophrenia. From late December 1977 to late January 1978, Chase killed six people in California because he thought his blood was turning to powder. By drinking the blood of victims, Chase believed, he could replenish his own blood. Mullin killed

13 people in a four-month span extending from October 1972 to February 1973. He believed the killings were the only way to placate nature and prevent a calamitous earthquake from destroying California. Like Chase and Mullin, most psychotic killers are apprehended relatively quickly. Mental illness makes them incapable of taking steps necessary to avoid detection or, in many cases, oblivious to the very idea that what they are doing is wrong and that anyone might want to stop them.

Richard Chase

The vast majority of serial killers, by contrast, understand that murder is wrong and that they will be punished if caught. These killers aren't insane in a medical or legal sense. But they typically have what psychologists call a personality disorder, such as antisocial personality disorder (ASPD) or psychopathy. People with ASPD have no regard for the rights of others. They are habitually deceitful, irresponsible, and impulsive. They often behave aggressively and get into repeated trouble with the law. According to the National Institutes of Health, only 3.6 percent of the American population has ASPD.

Psychopathy, which is sometimes regarded as a severe form of ASPD, is rarer still, affecting just 1 percent of the population. Psychopaths are cunning, manipulative, and often superficially charming. They tend to have a highly inflated sense of self-worth. They fail to accept responsibility for their actions, have no empathy, and never feel guilt or remorse. In short, they lack a conscience. This makes psychopaths especially dangerous as serial killers—though it must be stressed that only a very small percentage of psychopaths ever go on to become murderers.

Serial killers come from all racial, ethnic, and socioeconomic backgrounds. So do their victims. There is, however, a significant gender disparity among serial murder victims. Seven in 10, according to FBI data, are female.

Recent cases of serial murder have been documented in countries as diverse as Austria and Australia, Colombia and China, Peru and Pakistan, South Korea, South Africa, and Syria. Serial murder is truly a global phenomenon. This book presents representative cases from the United States and Great Britain.

DAVID BERKOWITZ
THE SON OF SAM

The pudgy young man had just gotten into his parked car, a cream-colored Ford Galaxie, when a group of men brandishing guns converged on the vehicle. Shouts of "Freeze! Police!" pierced the stillness of the summer night. From the driver's side, New York City Police Department detective John Falotico pressed his service revolver against the young man's temple and ordered him out of the car.

"Now that I've got you," Falotico asked, "who have I got?"

"You know," the young man replied softly, a childlike smile lighting up his face.

"No I don't. You tell me," the detective demanded.

"I'm Sam."

Those two words carried immense significance. They meant that on this night—August 10, 1977—a months-long reign of terror gripping the nation's largest city had come to an end. On a quiet street in Yonkers, the NYPD had finally captured the serial killer known as "the Son of Sam." In a string of shootings targeting young women and couples, he'd slain six people and wounded seven. The killer, who in a letter to police had described himself as a monster, turned out to be a 24-year-old post office employee named David Berkowitz.

Berkowitz was born Richard David Falco. His mother, who was already raising a daughter as a single parent, put him up for adoption so that she could continue an affair with a married man. The baby was adopted by Nathan and Pearl Berkowitz, a childless, middle-class couple who lived in New York City's Bronx borough. David apparently wasn't close to his adoptive father, and their relationship grew strained after Pearl Berkowitz's death, from cancer, when David was still a young teen. Nathan Berkowitz remarried, and David didn't get along with his new wife.

When he was about 21, Berkowitz located his birth mother and half-sister, and he tried to establish a relationship with them. But that effort didn't work out to his satisfaction. He was disturbed to discover the circumstances of his birth and adoption.

Nor was Berkowitz able to navigate romantic relationships. In fact, he never had a girlfriend. His resentment of women simmered. "The girls call me ugly," Berkowitz wrote in a November 1975 letter to his father, who had moved to Florida, "and they bother me the most."

The month after writing that letter, Berkowitz would first attempt—unsuccessfully, as it turned out—to kill a woman. On Christmas Eve, armed with a hunting knife, he walked the streets near his father's old apartment in the Bronx. In separate incidents, he attacked two young women from behind. The first screamed and ran away. The other received a half-dozen stab wounds but survived.

Before turning to murder, David Berkowitz was a prolific arsonist. Berkowitz kept a diary in which he detailed all the fires he set. There were more than 1,400 entries from September 1974 to December 1975.

CASE FILE

Name: David Richard Berkowitz (born Richard David Falco)

Monikers: the Son of Sam; the .44 Caliber Killer

Born: June 1, 1953

Period of homicides: 1976–1977

Number of victims: 6 killed; 7 wounded

Captured: Aug. 10, 1977

Outcome of case: pled guilty; sentenced to six consecutive terms of 25 years to life; eligible for parole beginning 2002

Berkowitz decided that he needed a more efficient way to kill. In June 1976, he drove all the way to Texas to get a handgun that, he believed, would be difficult to trace back to him. It wasn't long before he used the gun, a .44-caliber Charter Arms Bulldog revolver.

In the early morning hours of July 29, 1976, Berkowitz spotted two young women in a car parked on a residential street in the Bronx. Jody Valenti had driven her friend Donna Tauria home after their night out at a dance club, and the two chatted for a while. When Tauria finally opened the door to get out, Berkowitz approached the car and began shooting. Tauria, 18, was killed. Her 19-year-old friend was hit in the leg but survived. Police knew the shooter had used a .44-caliber Bulldog—the handgun leaves distinctive markings on bullets—but had few other leads.

Berkowitz struck two more times in 1976, with both attacks coming in the borough of Queens. In October he shot at a couple inside a parked car, wounding a young man. In November he gunned down two young women walking on a residential street. Both women survived, though one was left paralyzed.

As yet, no one in the NYPD realized that a serial killer was at work. In part, this reflected strikingly dissimilar descriptions of the suspect provided by eyewitnesses to the different shootings. In part, it was attributable to a dearth of ballistics evidence. All the bullets from the second and third shootings were very badly mangled. Police had no way to determine whether they had been fired from the same type of gun, much less match them to the specific Bulldog revolver used in the first shooting.

The next attack, which occurred in Queens during the early morning hours of January 30, 1977, yielded neither eyewitnesses nor conclusive ballistics evidence. This shooting claimed the life of a 26-year-old woman who'd been sitting in a car with her fiancé.

Berkowitz resumed his murder spree six weeks later, on March 8. The victim, 19-year-old college student Virginia Voskerichian, was walking home from a subway station in Queens around 7:30 PM when Berkowitz shot her once at close range. This time, the bullet was minimally deformed. An NYPD ballistics expert compared it with a bullet recovered from the Tauria-Valenti shooting. Striations made by the rifling on the inside of the gun barrel matched. Both bullets had been fired from the same .44-caliber Charter Arms Bulldog revolver.

On March 10, New York City's mayor and police chief held a press conference in which they confirmed the existence of a serial shooter. They also announced the formation of Operation Omega, an NYPD task force dedicated to catching the murderer. The press quickly nicknamed the unknown gunman "the .44 Caliber Killer."

Berkowitz identified himself by a different moniker in a letter he left at the scene of his next murders. "I AM THE 'SON OF SAM,'" proclaimed the four-page missive, which was handwrit-

Police and spectators view the body of Virginia Voskerichian, murdered near her home on March 8, 1977.

ten in all capital letters. Addressed to a member of the Omega task force, the letter was found near the bodies of a young couple who had been shot around 3 AM on April 17 as they sat in a parked car in the Bronx. Police didn't disclose the chilling contents of the letter—it implied that the killer was acting at the behest of "Papa Sam," who needed blood—but details about a vampire-obsessed psychopath leaked to the *New York Daily News.*

On June 5, the *Daily News* published excerpts from another Son of Sam letter. This one had been mailed to columnist Jimmy Breslin. "Sam's a thirsty lad

and he won't let me stop killing until he gets his fill of blood," the letter said. "Mr. Breslin, sir, don't think that because you haven't heard from me for a while that I went to sleep. No, rather, I am still here. Like a spirit roaming the night. Thirsty, hungry, seldom stopping to rest; anxious to please Sam. I love my work."

The *Daily News* had obtained the consent of the NYPD before publishing the Breslin letter; investigators were hoping that a reader might identify the killer from some detail in the communication. But much of the Son of Sam media coverage can only be described

NOT KNOWING WHAT THE FUTURE
HOLDS I SHALL SAY FAREWELL AND
I WILL SEE YOU AT THE NEXT JOB.
OR SHOULD I SAY YOU WILL SEE
MY HANDIWORK AT THE NEXT JOB?
REMEMBER MS. LAURIA. THANK YOU.

IN THEIR BLOOD
AND
FROM THE GUTTER

"SAM'S CREATION" .44

HERE ARE SOME NAMES TO HELP YOU ALONG.
FORWARD THEM TO THE INSPECTOR FOR
USE BY N.C.I.C.:
"THE DUKE OF DEATH"
"THE WICKED KING WICKER"
"THE TWENTY TWO DISCIPLES OF HELL"
"JOHN 'WHEATIES' - RAPIST AND SUFF-
OCATER OF YOUNG GIRLS.

PS: J.B., PLEASE INFORM ALL THE
DETECTIVES WORKING THE
SLAYINGS TO REMAIN

A page from the killer's letter to police,
which appeared in the *Daily News*.

Post even ran a story suggesting that the song "Purple Haze" might hold important clues. One of its columnists claimed to have heard the phrase "Help me, Son of Sam" on enhanced audio of the 1967 Jimi Hendrix hit.

Incessant coverage of the Son of Sam boosted newspaper circulation and TV news ratings. But it also fueled public hysteria and complicated the police investigation. Worse still, it appears to have encouraged Berkowitz. By his own admission, he reveled in all the attention his crimes received. He kept a scrapbook with his favorite clippings and religiously watched the nightly news. He also got ideas from the media. When a tabloid writer speculated, with no evidence whatsoever, that the Son of Sam might be planning to strike all five of New York City's boroughs, Berkowitz did in fact decide to expand his "hunting grounds."

The seventh Son of Sam shooting came in the early morning hours of June 26, 1977. A young man and woman who had spent the night dancing at a Queens disco were sitting in their car when Berkowitz walked up to the passenger-side window and opened fire. The young woman was hit three times and the young man once, but they both lived.

By this point, some 200 detectives were working the Son of Sam case full time as part of the Omega task force. Uniformed cops and precinct officers

as irresponsible. Day after day, regardless of whether there were any new developments, the case figured prominently in TV news broadcasts and was splashed across the pages of newspapers. The *Daily News* and its rival tabloid, the *New York Post*, were especially noteworthy for their sensationalistic pieces. Idle speculation masqueraded as reporting. Were the attacks tied to the phases of the moon? Had the Mafia taken out a hit on the Son of Sam? The also joined the hunt. But the number of leads that had to be investigated was staggering. Every day, the task force's hotline received more than a thousand new tips. None panned out. It seemed that the police might never catch the Son of Sam. Fearful New Yorkers locked themselves in their homes after dark, leaving once-bustling nightclubs deserted. Many women cut their hair short and dyed it blond because of the killer's apparent preference for targeting young women with long, dark hair.

Stacy Moscowitz was a blonde who wore her hair short, but that didn't save her. Nor did the fact that she and her boyfriend, Robert Violante, remained in Brooklyn during their Saturday night date. Previously, the Son of Sam had struck only in Queens and the Bronx. But that changed around 2:30 AM on July 31, when Moscowitz and Violante, both 20 years old, were hit by a hail of gunfire as they sat in Violante's car in Brooklyn's Gravesend neighborhood. Moscowitz died from a head wound. Violante survived the attack but lost an eye.

Initially, it appeared that the Son of Sam would elude the police yet again. A couple days after the shooting, however, a Gravesend resident came forward and reported that she'd seen a man loitering in the neighborhood on the night of July 30–31. The man had removed a parking ticket from the windshield of his car

The front page of the *Daily News* from June 27, 1977, pictures Son of Sam victims Judy Placido and Sal Lupo. They were wounded by four .44 caliber bullets fired at close range while they sat in a car parked in Bayside, Queens.

before getting in and driving off. Detective Ed Zigo decided to track down every ticket issued in the area on the night of the Moscowitz-Violante shooting.

On August 10, Zigo and his partner headed to Yonkers to interview one David Berkowitz, who had received a

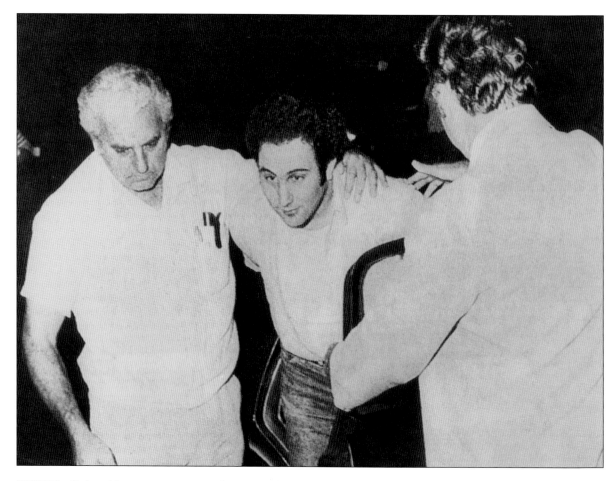

NYPD detectives escort a handcuffed David Berkowitz into police head-quarters in lower Manhattan, August 10, 1977.

citation for parking too close to a fire hydrant. The detectives located Berkowitz's Ford Galaxie, which was parked outside his apartment building. On the backseat, sticking out of a duffel bag, Zigo spotted the barrel of an assault rifle. Searching the car, he came across a letter addressed to the commander of the Omega task force. It promised a mass shooting at a disco. Zigo immediately phoned his superiors to report that the Son of Sam had been found.

Other detectives, including John Falotico, arrived at the scene. They decided to wait rather than risk a shootout by confronting Berkowitz in his apartment. After about six hours, Berkowitz emerged from the building and got into his car. The detectives swooped in for the arrest.

Once in custody, Berkowitz readily confessed to the shootings. He claimed that he'd been ordered to kill young, pretty women by his neighbor Sam Carr, who Berkowitz said was possessed by a 6,000-year-old demon. The orders to kill had been barked out by Carr's black Labrador retriever, which was also inhabited by a demon. Many psychiatrists believed that Berkowitz suffered from paranoid schizophrenia, and his lawyers wanted to mount an insanity defense. Instead Berkowitz pled guilty and, in June 1978, was sentenced to six consecutive life terms.

Robert Ressler, a pioneering FBI criminal profiler, interviewed Berkowitz extensively in prison. According to Ressler, Berkowitz admitted that he'd made up the whole story about receiving orders to kill from Sam Carr's demonically possessed dog. Berkowitz had wanted to dupe the authorities into believing he was insane. "He admitted that his real reason for shooting women," Ressler said, "was out of resentment toward his own mother, and because of his inability to establish good relationships with women." But Berkowitz would later tell yet another story: that he'd been part of a murderous satanic cult and had personally

Berkowitz used his .44-caliber Charter Arms Bulldog revolver to murder his victims.

pulled the trigger at only two Son of Sam shootings. Whether Berkowitz suffers from mental illness remains an open question.

Berkowitz first became eligible for parole in 2002. He was turned down then, and has been at every biennial parole hearing since. The man who shattered so many young lives in 1976 and 1977 seems destined to end his days behind bars.

TED BUNDY
CHARISMATIC KILLER

At a time when serial murder was little understood, many people thought it inconceivable that Ted Bundy might be capable of bludgeoning, raping, and killing dozens of young women. Bundy was intelligent, articulate, and charismatic. He projected empathy and consideration. He appeared to have a promising future in the law, or perhaps politics. In short, Bundy didn't seem at all like a monster. Even after he stood convicted of two brutal slayings and was suspected in more than 15 others, friends and acquaintances wondered whether there had been some mistake. "Everything I saw about him would recommend him," noted Ross Davis, for whom Bundy had worked when Davis was head of the Washington State Republican Party. "If you can't trust someone like Ted Bundy, you can't trust anyone—your parents, your wife, anyone."

Bundy did have a great ability to gain people's trust. He knew how to seem like a nice guy. But the reality couldn't have been more different. "I'm the most cold-blooded son of a bitch that you'll ever meet," he told a police detective in a moment of candor.

Bundy was born Theodore Robert Cowell on November 24, 1946. His mother, 22-year-old Eleanor Louise Cowell, was from Philadelphia but gave birth in a home for unwed mothers in Burlington, Vermont. Because of the stigma that was then attached to children born out of wedlock, her parents agreed to raise the baby as their own child. Bundy grew up believing that his mother, who went by the name Louise, was his older sister. Later, when he found out about this deception, he was indignant.

Bundy's grandfather appears to have been a violent and abusive man. In 1950

Louise decided to start a new life away from her family. She left Philadelphia with three-year-old Ted and went to live with relatives in Tacoma, Washington. Louise soon met Johnnie Bundy, a hospital cook. The two were married in May 1951, and Johnnie Bundy adopted his wife's four-year-old son. The couple would have four children together.

As he grew older, Ted became openly contemptuous of his stepfather. In his view, Johnnie Bundy wasn't smart or successful enough.

Otherwise, Ted Bundy seemed normal. Childhood friends knew him as funny and smart, though he could be somewhat aloof and at times displayed an explosive temper. Bundy, however, would say that for reasons he didn't fully comprehend, he became alienated from his friends when he entered high school. His social development stagnated. "I didn't know what made people want to be friends," Bundy later admitted to biographer Stephen Michaud. "I didn't know what made people attractive to one another. I didn't know what underlay social interactions."

Still, he earned good grades and was offered a small scholarship to the University of Puget Sound, located in Tacoma. He enrolled at UPS in the fall of 1965. The following year, he transferred to the University of Washington at Seattle as a Chinese major. At UW, for the first time in his life, he found a

CASE FILE

Name: Theodore Robert Bundy (born Theodore Robert Cowell)
Born: Nov. 24, 1946
Period of known homicides: 1974–1978
Number of victims: confessed to 30 murders; many investigators believe the actual number is 36 or more
Captured: Feb. 15, 1978
Outcome of case: convicted of three murders in Florida; sentenced to death
Died: Jan. 24, 1989 (executed in electric chair)

girlfriend. Bundy was absolutely smitten, and for a while the relationship went well. But the woman, tiring of what she considered Bundy's immaturity, dumped him after about a year. He was devastated. Unable to focus on his studies, he dropped out of college at the end of 1967.

Bundy got part-time jobs as a busboy and a supermarket stocker. Meanwhile, he began stealing and shoplifting, which he discovered he was quite good at. He had a knack for blending in and not drawing suspicion.

In 1968 Bundy volunteered for the campaign of Art Fletcher, a small-town

Republican politician who was running for lieutenant governor of Washington. Bundy impressed members of Fletcher's staff with his seriousness and competence, and he became the candidate's personal driver. During this time, apparently, Bundy greatly honed his skills at manipulating and charming people.

After Fletcher lost the election, Bundy left Washington. He went to Philadelphia, where in January 1969 he enrolled at Temple University. He took several theater classes, learning the basics of acting and discovering that his facial features were unusually indistinct. With a slightly different hairstyle or a bit of facial hair, Bundy could dramatically alter his appearance. This would serve him well in his career as a serial killer.

That career may have begun during Bundy's time at Temple. Shortly before his death, Bundy would tell an investigator that his first foray into murder involved the twin slayings of two women near Philadelphia. The incident to which he was alluding may have occurred over Memorial Day weekend in 1969, when two 19-year-old college students disappeared after eating at a diner in Somers Point, New Jersey. Their bodies were found a few days later in a wooded area near the Garden State Parkway. Both women had been stabbed to death. While Bundy is strongly suspected of the murders, the case may never officially be solved.

Bundy returned to Washington during the summer of 1969. In September, at a bar, he met a woman with whom he would have a long-term—if tempestuous—relationship. Elizabeth Kloepfer, divorced and the mother of a young daughter, worked as a secretary at the University of Washington's medical school. Bundy told Kloepfer he was a law student. Within three months, they had decided to get married. Then, abruptly, Bundy backed out, confessing that he'd lied about being a law student. Kloepfer forgave him.

In 1970 Bundy enrolled once again at the University of Washington. He majored in psychology; volunteered at the Seattle Crisis Clinic, answering calls to a suicide-prevention hotline; and graduated with honors in 1972. Throughout this time, Bundy habitually roamed the streets late at night, peeped into women's bedrooms, and on occasion broke into an apartment to steal a memento.

Bundy had decided that he really did want to go to law school. But, to his deep frustration, his scores on the Law School Admission Test weren't particularly good, and no law school accepted him.

However, in the summer of 1972, he went to work on another political campaign—the reelection bid of Washington's Republican governor, Daniel Evans—and again impressed his bosses. Evans and state Republican chairman Ross Davis wrote Bundy glowing letters of recommendation, and he was accepted into two law schools: at University of Utah and the University of Puget Sound. He chose the latter and was slated to start in the fall of 1973.

In the meantime, Bundy's Republican Party contacts helped him land jobs on the periphery of the criminal justice system. While working for the Seattle Crime Commission, Bundy helped research and write a report on rape prevention. He studied recidivism for the King County courts. He was proudest, however, of his job as an aide to Davis at the Washington GOP headquarters. Bundy used this position to impress the girlfriend who had jilted him six years before. While continuing his relationship with Kloepfer, he began dating this other woman. After he'd convinced her to marry him, Bundy unceremoniously dumped her.

In September 1973 Bundy entered the University of Puget Sound's law school with great expectations. He failed miserably. The UPS law program had only recently been established, and Bundy thought he belonged at a more prestigious institution. Nevertheless, he couldn't keep up with the coursework at UPS. He reapplied to the University of Utah College of Law as he struggled through a year at UPS.

The first killings that can definitively be tied to Bundy date to early 1974. On January 4 he broke into the basement apartment of an 18-year-old University

Many people were taken in by Ted Bundy's charm. They included Washington governor Daniel Evans (left) and state GOP chairman Ross Davis, for whom Bundy worked during the early 1970s.

of Washington student. As she lay sleeping, Bundy smashed her head with a metal rod and proceeded to sexually assault her. The woman suffered brain damage but survived.

On the night of January 31, Bundy carried out another savage attack on a sleeping woman. This time he abducted the victim, 21-one-year-old Lynda Ann Healy, after bludgeoning her. Healy's skull would be found about a year later at Taylor Mountain, a rugged, forested area in King County where Bundy dumped the remains of at least four of his other early victims. Like many other serial killers, Bundy took pleasure in revisiting the sites where he'd left his victims' bodies. Often he would bring eyeliner, rouge, and lipstick to make up the face of a woman he'd recently killed.

After the Healy murder, Bundy changed his modus operandi. Instead of

Bundy often dumped the bodies of his victims in wooded, hard-to-reach areas such as Taylor Mountain in Washington.

bludgeoning a victim as she slept, he began using his verbal skills and charm, often in combination with some ruse, to maneuver women into vulnerable positions. One favorite trick of his was to wear his arm in a sling or his leg in a cast and pretend to need help carrying something to his car. Another was to impersonate a security guard or police officer. Once Bundy got a victim into his car or alone in a secluded area, he would slap handcuffs on her or render her unconscious with a blow to the head from a crowbar. After sexually assaulting the victim, he would kill her, often by means of strangulation with a ligature.

By the early summer of 1974, police in Washington and Oregon were confronting a rash of disappearances of college women. In a creepy twist, Bundy landed a summer job at the Washington State Department of Emergency Services (DES). The responsibilities of the DES, which was located in Olympia, included searching for the women Bundy had abducted and killed.

During his months at the DES, Bundy succeeded in charming his colleagues, male and female alike. One coworker, Carole Boone, was especially attracted to the young law student. "I liked Ted immediately," Boone would recall. "We hit it off well. He struck me as being a rather shy person with a lot more going on under the surface than what was on the surface."

Elizabeth Kloepfer, too, had begun to suspect that there was a lot going on under the surface with Ted Bundy. At her boyfriend's apartment, Kloepfer had discovered a bag of women's clothes, along with plaster of paris mix and a pair of crutches. Later, she found a collection of keys in an eyeglass case of his. Kloepfer shuddered to think about what Bundy's possession of these things might signify. Her apprehension only increased after July 14, 1974.

That day, in separate incidents, two women disappeared from a beach at Lake Sammamish State Park, about 20 miles east of Seattle. Witnesses reported seeing 23-year-old Janice Ott accompany a handsome young man to his car, a brown Volkswagen. The man, who was wearing a tennis outfit, had one arm in a sling. Some four hours later and near the same spot, 19-year-old Denise Naslund left the beach to use a restroom. She never returned.

Police investigating the disappearances found five young women who all told a similar story. Each had been approached at Lake Sammamish by a man calling himself Ted, who was dressed in a tennis outfit and had his arm in a sling. He asked for help getting his sailboat from his car. Four of the women had refused outright; the fifth had accompanied Ted to his car, a brown VW, but had quickly fled when she noticed that there was no sailboat on it.

From the witness descriptions, a police artist produced a composite drawing of the suspect. It bore a certain resemblance to Ted Bundy. Colleagues

at the DES needled Bundy about this, and about the fact that he drove a brown VW. But they didn't seriously consider the possibility that Bundy was the suspect police sought in connection with the Lake Sammamish disappearances. Bundy was too nice a guy.

Elizabeth Kloepfer was less certain. Adding to her suspicions was a new look her boyfriend sported. Soon after area newspapers printed the police composite sketch, Bundy had gotten his hair cut very short. He looked like a completely different person. Kloepfer called a hotline police had set up in the case. Ultimately, however, she wouldn't identify her boyfriend or leave her own name.

In early September Bundy set out for Salt Lake City to attend law school at the University of Utah. En route, he picked up and killed a hitchhiker in Idaho. Her identity remains unknown.

Once at the University of Utah, Bundy quickly discovered that he was out of his depth academically. He fell hopelessly behind in his classes.

He soon resumed his killing, however. In October 1974, Bundy abducted and murdered a 16-year-old and two 17-year-olds in the Salt Lake area.

On November 8, he approached 18-year-old Carol DaRonch at a shopping mall near Midvale, Utah. He identified himself as a police officer and told DaRonch that someone had tried to break into her car. He asked her to accompany him to the nearby police station to file a complaint. DaRonch fell for the ploy. But soon after they'd set off in Bundy's Volkswagen, she realized that they were headed away from the police station. When she mentioned this, Bundy pulled to the side of the road and attempted to handcuff her. In the ensuing scuffle, however, he slapped both cuffs on the same wrist, and DaRonch managed to open the door and roll out of the car. Bundy, brandishing a crowbar, pursued her, but when DaRonch flagged down a passing car, Bundy returned to his VW and sped away.

Caryn Campbell

Debra Kent was not as fortunate. A few hours after DaRonch's harrowing escape, Bundy abducted Kent from the parking lot of her high school in Bountiful, Utah. The 17-year-old had been watching the school play with her parents but left to pick up her younger brother at a nearby roller rink.

As she read newspaper accounts of the abductions in Utah, Elizabeth Kloepfer became even more concerned about the possibility that her boyfriend was a killer. In late 1974 she contacted police in Washington and Utah and shared her suspicions. Investigators in Utah recorded Bundy's name for possible follow-up. In Washington, investigators decided to take a closer look at Bundy. Unfortunately, nothing in his background marked him immediately as a likely suspect. More important, when police administered a photo lineup, eyewitnesses from Lake Sammamish failed to recognize Bundy as the man calling himself Ted and requesting help with his sailboat.

By 1975 Bundy had expanded his hunting grounds. On January 12 he snatched Caryn Campbell, a 23-year-old nurse vacationing with her fiancé, from the hallway of a motel in Snowmass, Colorado. About a month later, Campbell's body was found a short distance away in a snowbank. In March Bundy murdered another woman in Vail, Colorado. In April he abducted and killed a bicyclist in Grand Junction, Colorado. His next known victim was a 12-year-old in the small town of Pocatello, Idaho. On May 6, Bundy lured the girl from her junior high school. He raped and killed her.

Bundy struck at least one more time—killing a 15-year-old in Provo, Utah, in late June—before his luck ran out. About 3 AM on August 16, Sergeant Bob Hayward, a highway patrol officer, was finishing his shift when he noticed a man sitting in a parked Volkswagen in his neighborhood in a Salt Lake City suburb.

When the officer turned on his flashing lights, the VW sped away. After a brief chase, Bundy pulled over at a gas station. He claimed he was lost. But in searching Bundy's car, Hayward found suspicious items such as rope, a crowbar, a ski mask made from pantyhose, handcuffs, and an ice pick. Bundy was arrested.

Under questioning, Bundy offered innocent explanations for having the odd items in his car. Police didn't believe him. Instead they assumed that the well-spoken law student was a would-be burglar. But when Salt Lake County detective Jerry Thompson heard about the arrest, he immediately thought of the attempted abduction of Carol DaRonch. Thompson also remembered Bundy's name in connection with Elizabeth Kloepfer's tip.

Investigating further, Thompson found evidence—including credit card receipts—that placed Bundy in or near the towns from which the three Colorado victims had been taken, and on the same days as their abductions. Thompson contacted police in Washington. He was informed that Bundy had emerged as a leading suspect in the serial murder investigation there.

In early October 1975, Bundy was subpoenaed to appear in a police lineup in Salt Lake City. Carol DaRonch immediately picked him out. So, also, did two witnesses from Bountiful who'd seen a stranger lurking at the back of the high school auditorium the night Debra Kent disappeared. Bundy was charged with aggravated kidnapping and assault in the DaRonch case. Though investigators were sure Bundy had abducted and killed Kent, they hadn't found her body and didn't believe they had sufficient evidence to bring charges.

The lead investigators in three states—Utah's Thompson, Bob Keppel of Washington, and Michael Fisher of Colorado—met in November 1975 to assess the case against Bundy. They agreed that Bundy was responsible for a large but unknown number of murders, though the evidence remained almost entirely circumstantial. A small army of investigators was marshaled to uncover hard evidence that would enable Bundy to be charged with specific killings.

Meanwhile, Bundy faced trial in the DaRonch kidnapping. He waived his right to a jury. Judge Stewart Hanson conducted the bench trial, which began on February 24, 1976. Reporters packed Hanson's Salt Lake City courtroom, and Bundy clearly enjoyed the spotlight. Taking the stand in his own defense, he sparred with prosecutor David Yocom, denying the charges with smug self-assurance. "You always sensed he thought he was smarter than anybody in the courtroom," Yocom recalled. But on March 1, Hanson found Bundy guilty of kidnapping and assault. He received a prison sentence of 1 to 15 years.

Bundy had served four months at Utah State Prison when officials in Colorado indicted him for the murder of Caryn Campbell. He decided to serve as his own lawyer in the case. On June 7, 1977, Bundy appeared at a preliminary hearing at the Pitkin County Courthouse in Aspen. During a recess in the proceedings, the judge allowed Bundy, under guard, to use the courthouse law library. Bundy managed to lull the guard into complacency. He wandered behind a bookshelf, then strode over to a window and leaped out, limping away from the two-story plunge with only a sprained ankle. Bundy was recaptured in Aspen six days later.

Incredibly, authorities failed to take special precautions to secure Bundy after this escape. Friends who visited

Bundy escaped from the Pitkin County Courthouse in Aspen by jumping out the second-floor window at the far left.

him at the Garfield County jail in Glenwood Springs—including his former coworker Carole Boone—smuggled money to him. Bundy also obtained a hacksaw blade, with which he cut a small hole in the ceiling of his cell. After losing 35 pounds, Bundy was able to fit through the one-square-foot opening. On the night of December 30, while most of the guards were on vacation, he squeezed through the hole, slithered along the crawl space above his cell, and broke through the ceiling of an unoccupied office. There he found, and changed into, civilian clothes. The man suspected of being one of the worst serial killers in U.S. history walked unnoticed out the front door of the jail.

No one realized that Bundy was gone until noon on December 31. By that time, Bundy was halfway across the country. He'd hitchhiked to Aspen, hopped a bus to Denver, and bought a plane ticket to Chicago.

Bundy was put on the FBI's Ten Most Wanted Fugitives list but managed to make his way—by train, stolen car, and bus—to Tallahassee, Florida. There, using a false name, he rented a room at a boardinghouse.

In the early morning hours of January 15, 1978, Bundy went on a monstrous rampage. He broke into a Florida State University sorority house and savagely attacked four women in their bedrooms. Bundy bludgeoned the victims with a piece of firewood. Two of them survived with serious injuries. Bundy strangled the other two, 21-year-old Margaret Bowman and 20-year-old Lisa Levy. After leaving the sorority house, Bundy attacked another Florida State student in her apartment several blocks away. She sustained multiple fractures to the face and skull but survived.

Three weeks later, Bundy stole a van and left Tallahassee. On February 9 he abducted 12-year-old Kimberly Diane Leach from her junior high in Lake City, Florida. He dumped her remains about 30 miles away.

Bundy abandoned the stolen van and headed west across the Florida Panhandle in a stolen Volkswagen. On February 15 a police officer in Pensacola pulled the VW over for a traffic violation. Upon running a license-plate check, the officer learned that the vehicle had been reported stolen, and he arrested the driver. However, it was only at the police station that the officer discovered, to his astonishment, that he'd collared Ted Bundy.

Bundy's trial for the murders of Margaret Bowman and Lisa Levy, along with related charges, opened in Miami on June 25, 1979. The atmosphere resembled a circus. Hundreds of print and TV reporters from across the globe were on hand. So, too, were scores of curiosity-seekers and swooning groupies, who acted as if Bundy were a

Florida State University students Lisa Levy (left) and Margaret Bowman were murdered by Ted Bundy in January 1978.

rock star rather than an accused killer. Bundy basked in all the attention. Ignoring the advice of his team of court-appointed attorneys, he represented himself—and in a sometimes histrionic fashion. But the law-school dropout proved no match for a seasoned prosecutor. Bundy couldn't undermine the testimony of an eyewitness who placed him outside the sorority house right after the murders, or the testimony of experts who matched bite marks on the body of one of the victims to the defendant's dentition. The jury deliberated just seven hours before returning guilty verdicts on July 23. Bundy was sentenced to death.

In his trial for the murder of Kimberly Leach, which began in January 1980, Bundy chose to entrust his defense to actual lawyers. The outcome was the same—he was found guilty and sentenced to death—but Bundy still

Ted Bundy in custody in Florida, 1978.

managed to indulge his vanity. During the penalty phase, while Carole Boone was on the stand testifying as a character witness on his behalf, Bundy asked her to marry him. She said yes.

Even after three murder convictions, Bundy continued to proclaim his innocence. Still, from death row at Florida State Prison in Raiford, he managed to set himself up as a kind of sage of serial murder. While he waited for his legal appeals to wend through the courts, Bundy sat down for many hours of interviews with journalists Stephen G. Michaud and Hugh Aynesworth. But he spoke in hypothetical terms and studiously used the pronoun "he" rather than "I" when discussing the mindset and methods of the serial killer who claimed victims in Washington, Utah, Colorado, and Florida. Bundy read articles by the FBI profiler Robert Ressler. He offered to provide his own insights into Washington State's Green River Killer—and in 1986 Bob Keppel and Green River task force member Dave Reichert took him up on the offer, traveling to Raiford and consulting at length with Bundy.

Bundy began to open up about his own murders only after his legal appeals were exhausted. In late 1988 he confessed to Keppel that, while police suspected him of 8 homicides in the Northwest, he'd actually committed 13. In January 1989 Bundy told William Hagmeier of the FBI's Behavioral Science Unit that he'd killed 30 victims in all. But many investigators believe that number wasn't a full accounting. Bundy had admitted to Keppel that there were some murders he would never discuss, and comments Bundy made in interviews with Michaud and Aynesworth appear to suggest that he first killed as an adolescent.

Bundy did, however, freely share

Many people celebrated the execution of Ted Bundy on January 24, 1989. This car—parked across the street from the Chi Omega House at Florida State University, where Bundy had killed two students—was photographed on the morning of the serial murderer's death.

many repugnant and chilling details of his behavior. He admitted to Hagmeier that he killed his victims to gain total possession of them. "You feel the last bit of breath leaving their body," Bundy said. "You're looking into their eyes . . . a person in that situation is *God!* You then possess them and they shall forever be a part of you. And the grounds where you kill them or leave them become sacred to you, and you will always be drawn back to them." The police investigators, psychiatrists, and journalists who interviewed Bundy were unanimous in concluding that he had no remorse whatsoever for his crimes.

In the days before Bundy's scheduled execution on January 24, 1989, detectives from Utah, Colorado, and Idaho flocked to Florida State Prison to interview him. Bundy hinted that he could help investigators locate victims' remains, and solve additional cases, if his execution was postponed. Bundy's lawyer urged the families of victims to petition Florida governor Bob Martinez to issue a stay of execution. None of the families responded. Martinez probably spoke for most of them when he characterized Bundy's attempt to bargain for more time as despicable. The governor refused to postpone the execution.

Guards and witnesses reported that the normally cocksure Bundy looked weak and frightened as he was led to the death chamber and strapped into the electric chair on the morning of January 24. At 7:15 AM, the current was turned on, and 2,000 volts of electricity coursed through Bundy's body. A minute later, the notorious serial killer was pronounced dead.

ANGELO BUONO JR. AND KENNETH BIANCHI

HILLSIDE STRANGLERS

Most serial killers carry out their crimes alone. On occasion, however, two depraved individuals will form a serial murder team. Such was the case with Angelo Buono Jr. and Kenneth Bianchi, adoptive cousins drawn together by a mutual hatred of women. In late 1977 and early 1978, the two raped, tortured, and murdered 10 girls and young women in Los Angeles. Most of the victims died by strangulation, and their bodies were dumped in the hills surrounding L.A. Those facts, along with the incorrect assumption that one person was responsible for the killings, led local media to confer the moniker "the Hillside Strangler."

Buono was born in Rochester, New York. At the age of five, he moved with his mother and sister to Glendale, a suburb of Los Angeles, following his parents' divorce. He appears to have despised his mother.

As a teenager, Buono was sent to a juvenile detention facility for stealing a car. But the experience didn't turn him away from further law breaking. Even before his descent into murder, Buono had compiled an extensive criminal record, with offenses ranging from auto theft to assault to rape.

In spite of his recurring troubles with the law, Buono married a total of five times between 1955 and 1972. He fancied himself quite the lothario, but in his relationships he invariably gave vent to his need to dominate, humiliate, and inflict pain on women. Buono's sadism (and, in at least one case, his sexual abuse of a stepdaughter) eventually broke up all his marriages. By 1976—around the time he met Kenneth Bianchi—Buono was living alone in a Glendale house that doubled as the office for his automobile upholstery business.

Bianchi, 16 years Buono's junior, had also been born in Rochester. His birth mother, a teenaged prostitute, didn't want him, and he was adopted by Angelo Buono's aunt and uncle. They had no other children. According to his adoptive mother, Bianchi displayed behavior problems from early childhood. He lied compulsively, was highly manipulative, and got into trouble in school.

Still, Bianchi was intelligent, and he managed to graduate from high school. Shortly afterward, he wed his high school girlfriend. The marriage lasted only slightly longer than Bianchi's one-semester college career. He'd wanted to obtain a degree that would help him realize his lifelong dream of becoming a police officer, but had flunked out instead. Bianchi settled for a series of jobs as a store security guard. He was fired from several of those jobs for theft.

In late 1975 or early 1976, Bianchi headed to California to live with his older cousin Angelo Buono. He soon found a job at a real estate title company, but he also applied to the Los Angeles and Glendale police departments. His applications were rejected. For a while, Bianchi rented office space

CASE FILE

Name: Angelo Buono Jr.
Born: Oct. 5, 1934
Period of homicides: Oct. 1977–Feb. 1978
Number of victims: 10
Captured: Oct. 19, 1979
Outcome of case: convicted of nine counts of murder; sentenced to nine life terms without parole
Died: Sept. 21, 2002

CASE FILE

Name: Kenneth Alessio Bianchi
Born: May 22, 1951
Period of homicides: Oct. 1977–Jan. 1979
Number of victims: 12
Captured: Jan. 12, 1979
Outcome of case: pled guilty to seven murders; sentenced to eight life terms

and represented himself as a licensed psychologist. Though he had the superficial charm, talent for deception, and highly exaggerated sense of self-worth characteristic of psychopaths, Bianchi failed to attract many patients to his phony counseling practice.

He did, however, attract a woman he'd met at the title company. Bianchi eventually moved out of Buono's house and moved in with her. After she became pregnant, Bianchi proposed marriage. She declined, though they continued to live together.

Behind the façade of a stable relationship, Bianchi seethed with contempt for women. That contempt came to the fore under the influence of Buono. The cousins lured several young runaways to Buono's house. There the girls were beaten, abused, and forced into prostitution.

Buono and Bianchi decided that the quickest and best way to build their pimping operation was to get a list of clients from an experienced prostitute. They bought such a list from a local prostitute but soon discovered, to their fury, that the names were phony. Buono and Bianchi couldn't find the prostitute who had scammed them. They did, however, find her friend, 19-year-old Yolanda Washington. They abducted, raped, and brutally beat Washington before strangling her with a cloth. Washington's body, laid out in a provocative pose, was discovered near a cemetery in Hollywood Hills on October 18, 1977.

The cousins had committed their first murder as an act of revenge. But they had enjoyed the experience, and in the weeks that followed, they went on a killing spree. Their modus operandi was to get a victim into their car—often by impersonating police officers—and drive to Buono's house. There they would rape, torture, and kill the victim, usually by strangling her with a ligature. Then they would clean the body to get rid of potential evidence. Buono and Bianchi made little effort to prevent the bodies of their victims from being discovered. In fact, most of the bodies were dumped near busy places—for example, in residential neighborhoods, along a freeway off-ramp, on a hill close to Dodger Stadium. In doing this, criminal profilers suggest, Buono and Bianchi were taunting the police, to whom they felt superior.

By late November, seven more bodies had been found. Other than their youth—only one was over 22—the victims didn't appear to have much in common. They included a prostitute, a waitress, a high school senior, and an aspiring actress. Two victims, schoolgirls aged 12 and 14, had been abducted together shortly after getting off their bus. Twenty-year-old Kristina Weckler was an art and design student in college. Weckler happened to live in the same Glendale apartment complex as Bianchi and his girlfriend.

The local media blared warnings about "the Hillside Strangler," but police were confident a pair of psychopaths was at work. Witnesses reported seeing the schoolgirls approach two men in a parked car right before they went missing. Another victim was seen arguing with two men in a car the night she disappeared.

The Los Angeles and Glendale police departments, joined by the Los Angeles County Sheriff's Department, formed a task force to stop the killers. However, Buono and Bianchi struck again in December, murdering a prostitute and dumping her body on a hillside just a few feet from a residential street.

In February 1978, the body of 20-year-old Cindy Hudspeth was found in the trunk of her car. The vehicle had plunged into a deep ravine, apparently after being pushed off the highway above. At first blush, the case didn't seem related to the Hillside Strangler murders. The bodies of all nine previous victims had been dumped in the open. But ligature marks on Hudspeth's body were similar to those found on other victims, and task force investigators correctly concluded that she, too, had been killed by the unknown pair of serial killers. Hudspeth's apartment in Glendale was right across the street

Members of the Hillside Strangler task force in the ravine where Cindy Lee Hudspeth's car was found. The victim's leg is visible in the trunk.

Kenneth Bianchi testifies against his cousin and accomplice Angelo Buono in November 1981.

from the apartment building of Kristina Weckler (and Kenneth Bianchi). While investigators could find no evidence the two women had ever met, they were now convinced that at least one of the killers lived in Glendale.

After the Hudspeth slaying, the Hillside Strangler murders abruptly stopped. The explanation, police would only later find out, was that the killer team had broken up. In March 1978, Bianchi's girlfriend left him, taking their infant son and moving to Bellingham, Washington, to live with her parents. Bianchi soon convinced her to take him back, and he left Glendale for Bellingham.

There he got a job as a guard with a

security agency. He also took courses in police science and applied for a position with the local sheriff's department. None of that meant that Bianchi had lost his taste for murder. In January 1979, he offered a former coworker, Karen Mandic, and her college roommate $100 apiece to watch a secluded—and temporarily unoccupied—home for two hours one night while its alarm system was being fixed. Bianchi asked that the women not tell anyone about the house-sitting job. But Mandic mentioned the assignment, along with Bianchi's name, to several friends. So when the bodies of the two women were found in the backseat of Mandic's car, the police investigation quickly focused on Bianchi.

Noting the address on the suspect's California driver's license, a Bellingham police detective telephoned authorities in Glendale for information about Kenneth Bianchi. By chance, this call was directed to a detective who had worked on the since-disbanded Hillside Strangler task force. He was intrigued to learn that the murder victims in Washington had been strangled by ligature. But what really caught his attention was Bianchi's old address. Could it be a coincidence that two Hillside Strangler victims had lived on the same block as a man now implicated in murders carried out in a similar manner? The possibility seemed even more remote after a search of Bianchi's Bellingham home turned up a distinctive necklace and ring. Those items matched jewelry missing from two of the Hillside Strangler victims.

Angelo Buono Jr.

Los Angeles police began trying to put together a case against Bianchi in the Hillside Strangler killings. Meanwhile, he was charged with two counts of first-degree murder in the Bellingham slayings. Bianchi's lawyer entered a plea of not guilty by reason of insanity, saying psychiatrists had found that his client suffered from multiple-personality disorder (now called "dissociative identity disorder"). When Bianchi was put under hypnosis, an alternate identity, "Steve Walker," supposedly emerged. "Walker" not only admitted killing Karen Mandic and her roommate, but also confessed to carrying out the Hillside Strangler murders with Angelo Buono.

After a court-appointed psychiatrist and expert in hypnosis concluded that Bianchi was faking his multiple personalities, Bianchi accepted a deal. Prosecutors agreed not to pursue the death penalty. In exchange, Bianchi agreed to plead guilty to the two Bellingham murders and five of the Hillside Strangler murders, in addition to testifying against Buono. Bianchi received two life sentences in Washington and six life sentences in California.

On the morning of October 19, 1979, minutes after his cousin's guilty plea in Washington, Buono was arrested at his home in Glendale. Pretrial hearings consumed months—and the entire case against Buono seemed on the verge of collapsing when Bianchi recanted his testimony. But the trial finally began in November 1981. It lasted more than two years, but ultimately the jury convicted Buono of 9 of the 10 Hillside Strangler murders. He was sentenced to nine life terms, without possibility of parole.

Buono died of a heart attack in 2002. Bianchi remains in a prison in Washington State. He won't be eligible for parole until 2059. In the unlikely event that he is still alive at age 108, parole will simply mean transfer to the California prison system to serve out six more life sentences.

ED GEIN
SHY PSYCHO

Psycho, Alfred Hitchcock's 1960 classic, has horrified generations of cinema fans. Its creepy main character, Norman Bates, was inspired by a real-life serial murderer named Ed Gein. Gein also served as a model for the character Buffalo Bill, the serial killer who skins his victims in the 1991 thriller *The Silence of the Lambs*.

Edward Gein grew up on farm in Plainfield, Wisconsin. He had a troubled childhood. His father, George, was an abusive alcoholic who couldn't hold a job. His mother, Augusta, was a religious fanatic who constantly ridiculed her husband and berated Ed and his older brother, Henry. Augusta Gein carped about her sons' every shortcoming—of which she found many—and predicted that they would turn out like their worthless father. She warned the boys continually about the fires of hell. Women, she said, were the surest path to eternal damnation. They were wicked and immoral, and Ed and Henry were never to associate with them.

If women represented a special menace, Augusta Gein saw sinners everywhere. To shield her sons from corrupting influences, she prevented them from forming any friendships. The Gein brothers grew up profoundly isolated on the family farm, where both remained after reaching adulthood.

In a five-year period, Ed Gein lost his entire family. His father died from pneumonia in 1940. Henry died four years later in a fire. But for Ed Gein the hardest blow of all came in 1945, when his mother succumbed after a series of strokes. With her death, one writer noted, the 39-year-old Gein "had lost his only friend and one true love."

Gein stayed on the farm. To support himself, he did odd jobs for neighbors. People around Plainfield knew him as quiet, shy, and slightly eccentric. In fact, he was more than slightly eccentric.

Gein had taken to digging up the graves of recently deceased women, beginning with his own mother. He removed skin and body parts, which he took home to keep as fetish objects or fashion into household items, including bowls made from skulls, a lampshade consisting of a face, and a belt made of nipples. Gein created a woman's jumpsuit made entirely of skin. Its accompanying vest had breasts. Gein wore the suit periodically in a transvestite ritual. Confused by his abnormal relationship with his mother, he apparently wanted to turn himself into a woman.

By 1954 Gein had graduated from grave robbing to murder. In December of that year, he shot Mary Hogan, a local tavern keeper who Gein thought bore a strong physical resemblance to his mother. He carved up Hogan's body at his farmhouse. Three years later, in 1957, Gein shot the owner of a Plainfield hardware store, Bernice Worden. This time, police quickly linked him to the crime. Upon searching his farmhouse, they found Worden's headless corpse, along with body parts from more than a dozen other women. Gein admitted to killing only Worden and Hogan, insisting that all the other body parts had come from the graves

Ed Gein

CASE FILE

Name: Edward Theodore Gein
Born: Aug. 27, 1906
Period of homicides: 1954–1957
Number of victims: 2
Captured: Nov. 16, 1957
Outcome of case: convicted of one count of murder, but ruled insane; place in mental hospital
Died: July 26, 1984

he'd dug up. Police suspected him in a handful of missing-persons cases in the area, but no proof was ever found.

Gein was deemed not competent to stand trial. Psychiatrists who examined him diagnosed schizophrenia, and he was committed to a state mental hospital for the criminally insane.

A decade later, however, doctors pronounced Gein mentally competent to stand trial. In a weeklong trial in November 1968, he was found guilty of the murder of Bernice Worden. But the court ruled him insane at the time of the slaying, and Gein was sent back to the mental hospital, where he spent the rest of his life. He died from cancer on July 26, 1984.

A policeman finds the body of one of Jack the Ripper's victims in London's Whitechapel district, 1888.

JACK THE RIPPER

He ranks as history's most famous serial killer, a fiend who in 1888 haunted London's Whitechapel district. He preyed on prostitutes, slitting his victims' throats and then hideously mutilating their bodies, which he posed provocatively and left in places where they would readily be found. Newspapers of the day were filled with shocking accounts of the crimes, and countless volumes about the case have been written in the 125 years since. Yet very little can be said with certainty about the notorious killer—not even whether he actually wrote the taunting letter that gave rise to his gruesome nickname: Jack the Ripper.

London in 1888 was the world's most populous city, with approximately 4.3 million inhabitants. The seat of Britain's government and the administrative and commercial center of its far-flung empire, London was a bastion of power and privilege. The City—a square-mile section of old London—boasted the greatest concentration of wealth on the planet.

But there was another side of London. In the teeming slums of the East End, immigrants, the homeless, and the poor struggled to eke out a meager daily existence. Women were among the most vulnerable. Thousands turned to prostitution, selling sex to pay for food, alcohol, or a bed in one of the dilapidated lodging houses that dotted the East End.

The Whitechapel district, though it abutted the City, was among the East End's most squalid sections. Perhaps not surprisingly, violence against women was fairly common in Whitechapel. That fact helps explain why it's not entirely certain when Jack the Ripper began his murderous spree,

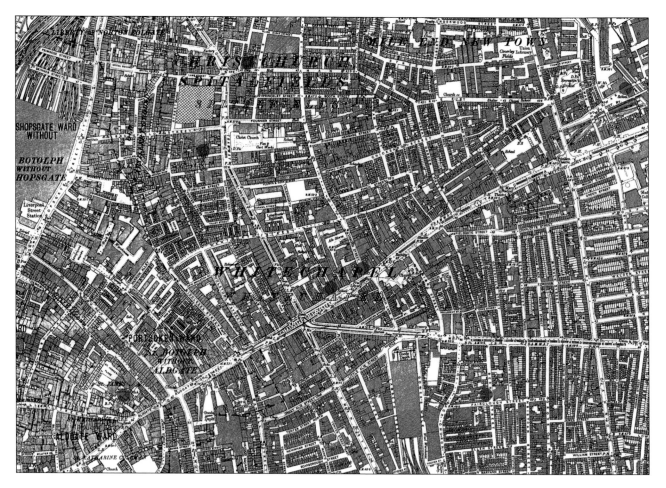

This 1894 map shows the locations of six of the eleven "Whitechapel Murders" committed between 1888 and 1891. Jack the Ripper is believed to have committed five of those killings.

or when the spree ended. Scotland Yard—as London's Metropolitan Police is popularly known—investigated 11 possibly linked killings as part of its "Whitechapel Murders" file. Those homicides occurred between April 1888 and February 1891. Today, however, most authorities believe that the Ripper killed five women, from August to November 1888.

The first of those victims was Mary Ann "Polly" Nichols. The 43-year-old mother of five had become a prostitute

after her husband left her. Around 3:40 AM on August 31, a cart driver found Nichols's body lying on the pavement of Buck's Row, a dark, narrow street in Whitechapel. Her throat had been slashed so savagely that Nichols was nearly decapitated. The victim's abdomen had also been cut.

Police could find no witnesses to the murder. However, upon questioning area prostitutes, they learned that a mysterious man had been verbally abusing and threatening streetwalkers for months. The prostitutes said the man was foreign born and, probably, Jewish. They had nicknamed him "Leather Apron," from the article of clothing he was always seen wearing. Scotland Yard focused on finding Leather Apron, considering him the prime suspect in the murder of Polly Nichols, as well as the earlier slaying of another prostitute. The investigation was greatly complicated when, on September 5, a local newspaper called the *Star* ran a lurid story linking the shadowy character known as Leather Apron to the Whitechapel murders. It would be the first of many instances in which sensational press coverage hindered the chances of catching Jack the Ripper.

The next Ripper slaying followed

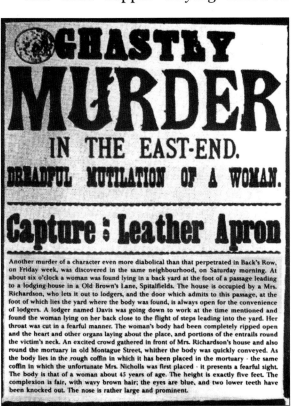

CASE FILE

Name: Jack the Ripper
Period of homicides: Sept.–Nov. 1888
Number of victims: generally accepted as 5
Outcome of case: never solved

close on the heels of the *Star*'s Leather Apron story. Like Polly Nichols, the new victim, 45-year-old Annie Chapman, had fallen on hard times after separating from her husband. Chapman cobbled together a precarious livelihood by sewing, by selling flowers, and through prostitution. She had no money to pay for a bed at a lodging house on September 8, so she walked the streets of Whitechapel's Spitalfields neighborhood. Around 5:30 AM, a witness saw her talking to a short, swarthy man who had a shabby but genteel appearance. A half hour later, Chapman's body was found in the backyard of a three-story brick building in Spitalfields. The killer

(Left) A newspaper report about the Ripper's second murder—the killing of Annie Chapman (right).

had slashed her throat, cut open her abdomen, and thrown her intestines over her shoulders.

Three weeks later, Scotland Yard received a letter purporting to be from the killer. Dated September 25 and written neatly in red ink, the two-page communication (which included multiple errors in punctuation) had been mailed to the Central News Service. "Dear Boss," the letter began.

> I keep on hearing the police have caught me but they wont fix me just yet. . . . That joke about Leather Apron really gave me fits. I am down on whores and shant quit ripping them till I do get buckled. Grand work the last job was. I gave the lady no time to squeal. How can they catch me now. I love my work and want to start again. . . . The next job I do I shall clip the ladys ears off and send to the police officers just for jolly wouldn't you.

The letter was signed "Jack the Ripper."

Some police detectives thought the "Dear Boss" letter was a hoax, probably by a reporter looking to boost newspaper circulation. Initially, Scotland Yard decided to withhold the missive from the public.

That decision would be reversed after the murderer struck next. In the early morning hours of September 30, two prostitutes—44-year-old Elizabeth Stride and 46-year-old Catherine Eddowes—were slain. Stride's body was found in a yard in Whitechapel. Her throat had been slit but otherwise there was no mutilation, possibly because the killer had been interrupted. Eddowes, too, had died as a result of having her throat slashed, but the postmortem disfigurement was horrifying. Her face had been extensively deformed, and the killer had cut open her abdomen, pulling out the intestines and tossing them over her shoulder. The left kidney and uterus were missing. Eddowes's body was found in Mitre Square. This was just inside the limits of the City, which had its own police department. The City of London Police thus joined Scotland Yard in investigating the Ripper murders, but the rival departments generally failed to cooperate.

Two officials with Scotland Yard, Commissioner Charles Warren and Police Superintendent Thomas Arnold, made a controversial decision in the first hours after the September 30 murders. A bloody piece of Catherine Eddowes's apron, which the killer apparently carried away from Mitre Square, was found near the doorway of a tenement house on Goulston Street in Whitechapel. Above the doorway,

Charles Warren

written in chalk, was a cryptic graffito. Recollections would differ slightly, but it read something like, "The Juwes are The men that Will not be Blamed for nothing." Had the killer written this message? Or was it simply a coincidence that he'd dropped the piece of Eddowes's apron below it? Warren and Arnold couldn't be sure, but they interpreted "Juwes" as a misspelling of "Jews." Anti-Semitism had been running strong in Whitechapel since Leather Apron's identification as a Jew. Fearing a riot targeting Jews, Warren and Arnold ordered the graffito washed off before it could be photographed. A clue in the Ripper case may thereby have been lost.

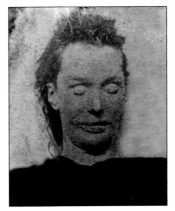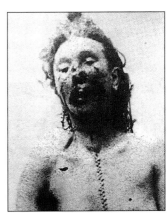

Victims of the Ripper's "double event" on September 30, 1888: Elizabeth Stride (left) and Catherine Eddowes, whose torso has been stitched together.

On October 1, Scotland Yard decided to release the text of the "Dear Boss" letter, in part because one of Eddowes's ears had been cut off (though it was found near the body, not sent to police, as the letter had promised). Police were hoping someone might recognize the writer. Hundreds of people thought they did, flooding Scotland Yard with tips. None panned out. Hundreds of other letters claiming to be from Jack the Ripper were sent to the police and to news organizations, though almost all of these were clearly hoaxes.

One possible exception was a postcard sent to the Central News Agency and postmarked October 1. Like the "Dear Boss" letter, it was written in red ink—with similar if not identical handwriting—and signed Jack the Ripper. "I was not codding dear old Boss when I gave you the tip," the postcard read, "you'll hear about Saucy Jacky's work tomorrow double event this time number one squealed a bit couldn't finish straight off. ha not the time to get ears for police. thanks for keeping last letter back till I got to work again." The "double event" seemed a clear reference to the Stride and Eddowes killings, which hadn't yet been reported in the newspapers at the time the postcard was sent. For this reason, many investigators thought the postcard—and hence the "Dear Boss" letter—were genuine communications from the killer. Other investigators disagreed, pointing out that if the postcard writer lived or worked in Whitechapel, he could well have heard about the Stride-Eddowes

The first page of the "Dear Boss" letter, which may have been written by the killer to taunt police.

murders by the following morning. And the other details, such as the pseudonym Jack the Ripper, would have been available from the "Dear Boss" letter, which was published in a local newspaper early on October 1. Alternatively, the same hoaxer could have written both the "Dear Boss" letter and the "Saucy Jacky" postcard. Today, expert opinion on the authenticity of the two communications remains divided.

October 1888 passed with no further murders in Whitechapel. Nevertheless, panic over Jack the Ripper gripped the East End and, for that matter, all of London. That panic was fanned by sensationalistic—and in many cases false—newspaper coverage of the case. Metropolitan Police officials absorbed withering criticism for their supposed ineptitude. In reality, Scotland Yard conducted an investigation that, for the time, was almost unprecedented in scope. Police detectives interviewed more than 2,000 people. They investigated about 300 suspects in depth. Convinced the killer lived in Whitechapel, they carried out a house-to-house search of the district. Several dozen people were taken into custody, but all were eventually released.

Meanwhile, among the deluge of Jack the Ripper letters that police had to evaluate, one stood out as another possible communication from the killer. It was received on October 16 by George Lusk, chairman of the Whitechapel Vigilance Committee, a group of citizen volunteers who'd begun patrolling the district's streets each night. The letter, which was riddled with mistakes, read in full:

> From hell
> Mr Lusk
> Sor
> I send you half the Kidne I took from one woman and prasarved it for you tother piece I fried and ate it was very nise. I may send you the bloody knif that took it out if you only wate a whil longer
>   signed
> Catch me when you can Mishter Lusk

Along with the letter was a box containing part of a kidney, which had been preserved in spirits. An eminent surgeon who examined the organ concluded that it had come from a human and was part of a left kidney. But, because the techniques of modern forensic science were unknown in the late 19th century, the kidney couldn't definitively be matched to Catherine Eddowes. Of course, that didn't stop London newspapers from proclaiming that the kidney had indeed been cut out of the latest Ripper victim.

Soon, however, the papers had another murder to report. The victim, Mary Kelly, was a prostitute of about 25. Shortly before midnight on November 8, Kelly took a hefty, ginger-haired man into her room in a lodging house located in one of Whitechapel's most notorious areas. The following morning, Kelly's body was found on her bed. The mutilation was even more ghastly than with previous Ripper victims. Most of Kelly's face was gone. Skin and muscle had been stripped from a large portion of the body, and internal organs had been removed and arranged on the bed. The heart was missing.

Mary Kelly is widely—but not universally—regarded as Jack the Ripper's fifth and final victim. Other prostitute murders in the area of Whitechapel failed to include the Ripper's signature mutilation and so, in the view of most criminologists, probably weren't his work. Still, it is impossible to say with certainty, as the killer was never caught.

In any event, the panic that engulfed the East End in late 1888 gradually receded. Yet fascination with Jack the Ripper has never waned. Over the years, diverse theories of the case have been offered by a seemingly endless parade of authors, from armchair detectives and amateur profilers to careful historians and experienced criminal investigators. A small sampling:

- A young teacher named Montague John Druitt was Jack the Ripper. Druitt, considered one of just a handful of serious suspects by Scotland Yard, committed suicide in December 1888.

- Prince Albert Victor, Duke of Clarence and Avondale, was Jack the Ripper. Eddy, as the prince was called, was rumored to frequent seedy areas of London and to be insane from syphilis.

- The Ripper murders were a conspiracy to protect the British monarchy from embarrassment. Prince Albert Victor, according to the theory, had fathered a child with (and may have secretly married) a lower-class woman in

Some who have been suspected of being Jack the Ripper include Prince Albert Victor (left) and Montague John Druitt. However, the actual identity of the murderer will probably never be known.

Whitechapel. The Ripper victims were killed because they knew about Eddy's affair. The conspiracy involved the British prime minister, Lord Salisbury; Queen Victoria's personal physician, Sir William Gull; and Gull's coachman, John Netley. Top police officials may also have been involved.

- The Ripper was a woman, which explains how the killer slipped away from crime scenes without arousing suspicion. This "Jill the Ripper" is variously suggested to have been a crazed midwife, an abortionist, or a lesbian.

- Jack the Ripper was the artist Walter Sickert, who regularly used prostitutes as models and who painted a series of canvases depicting or inspired by the murder of a prostitute.

None of these theories—or any of the hundred or so others that have been proposed—is entirely convincing. Some are clearly outlandish. Others are intriguing but suffer from contradictory, ambiguous, or missing evidence. Still others rely on speculation.

Every few years, it seems, another author emerges with a book or paper that proclaims to definitively identify Jack the Ripper. Invariably, however, the case falls apart on close examination. Who really perpetrated history's most famous serial murders might never be known.

HERMAN W. MUDGETT
DR. H.H. HOLMES

For six months in 1893, people flocked to Chicago to visit the World's Columbian Exposition. Built amid canals and lagoons, the exposition's main grounds—dubbed the White City—was a wonderland of neoclassical architecture, monumental sculpture, elegant promenades, and lovely vistas. But organizers were interested in more than just creating a beautiful setting. They hoped to showcase American technological and commercial prowess and illustrate the "progress of civilization." In this regard, the Chicago World's Fair did not disappoint. Visitors marveled at the moving sidewalk and the elevated train. They witnessed demonstrations of the telephone and phonograph. They rode the world's first Ferris wheel, a 260-foot-high behemoth that carried more than 2,100 passengers at a time. In all, the Columbian Exposition's many attractions drew about 27 million visitors between May 1 and October 30.

Some of those visitors found lodging at a hotel a few miles west of the White City. To capitalize on tourism surrounding the Columbian Exposition, the three-story, block-long structure was named the World's Fair Hotel. Because of its fortress-like appearance, however, locals called it "the Castle." The nickname was appropriate for another reason, one that nobody at the time could have suspected. Deep within the Castle, in windowless and soundproof rooms, victims suffered agonizing deaths that rivaled the torment inflicted in medieval dungeons. The proprietor of the World's Fair Hotel, who called himself Dr. H. H. Holmes, is among America's first documented serial murderers.

H. H. Holmes was born Herman Webster Mudgett in the small town of Gilmanton, New Hampshire. Details

CASE FILE

Name: Herman Webster Mudgett

Alias: Dr. H. H. Holmes

Born: 1861?

Period of homicides: 1887?–1894

Number of victims: estimates range from 27 to 200

Captured: Nov. 17, 1894

Outcome of case: convicted of four counts of murder, sentenced to death

Died: May 8, 1896 (executed by hanging)

about his early life are sketchy. By all accounts, though, he was highly intelligent.

Mudgett attended medical school at the University of Michigan but was expelled, apparently for stealing cadavers. He drifted around the Midwest for a brief period before appearing in Chicago as Dr. H. H. Holmes. There, in 1886, he parlayed his supposed medical degree into a job as a druggist at a thriving drugstore. Before long, Holmes had arranged to purchase the business from its owner, an elderly widow. He was to pay her in installments, but she disappeared soon after the sale. It is assumed that Holmes killed her in order to avoid paying his debt.

Holmes grew rich on the profits from his drugstore. He became involved in other lucrative ventures, many of them shady if not completely fraudulent. As a con man, he was remarkably talented. Women found him especially charming, and he took full advantage. Holmes bilked several out of their fortunes. He would eventually be married to three women, and perhaps more, at the same time.

After buying a parcel of land near his drugstore, Holmes began construction of what would become the World's Fair Hotel. He designed the building himself. Its many odd features included hidden passageways, twisting hallways that led nowhere, windowless bedrooms lined with fire-retarding asbestos, doors that could be opened only from the outside, rooms that were accessible through trapdoors or sliding walls, and chutes from the upper floors to the basement.

As the edifice was being built, Holmes replaced construction managers and crews regularly. This was to ensure that no one understood the building's bizarre layout or knew about all of its odd fittings. With that information, a keen observer might have deduced the hidden purpose of the structure: to facilitate its owner's penchant for torture and murder.

The World's Fair Hotel opened in 1893, just in time for the Columbian

Exposition. The guest accommodations, about 100 rooms in all, were on the second and third floors. The second floor also contained Holmes's personal office. His drugstore and other shops were on the first floor.

On many days, Holmes left his office and went to the exposition grounds. Sometimes he took with him the children of Benjamin Pitezel, a carpenter who had worked on the Castle. In the White City or the Midway Plaisance—the Columbian Exposition's center of entertainment and shopping—Holmes would strike up conversations with tourists. He would invite them to his hotel. For many, especially young women who were traveling alone, accepting Holmes's invitation would prove to be a fatal decision.

Once inside the Castle, Holmes's guests were completely at his mercy—and mercy was a quality about which he knew nothing. Holmes locked some victims inside an airtight safe in his office, allowing them to suffocate only feet away from where he blithely worked. He pumped gas into the airtight and asbestos-lined bedrooms in which other victims were lodged. Through a peephole, Holmes would watch as the victim died, either by asphyxiation or by fire, if Holmes decided to ignite the gas. Other victims met an agonizing end on the "elasticity determinator"—Holmes's version of the medieval rack. The full

View of the Midway Plaisance at the 1893 World's Columbian Exposition in Chicago. Holmes frequently visited the exposition grounds to lure potential victims to his hotel.

variety of horrors Holmes devised can only be conjectured.

Holmes dropped his victims' bodies into the chutes that led to the hotel basement. There, he incinerated some in a specially designed kiln. Others were dissolved in a vat of acid. Holmes dissected and stripped the flesh from still other bodies, selling organs and skeletons to medical schools.

Not all of Holmes's victims were guests of his hotel. Some were employees. Holmes bought life insurance policies for his workers, with himself as the beneficiary. He poisoned an unknown number of employees for the insurance.

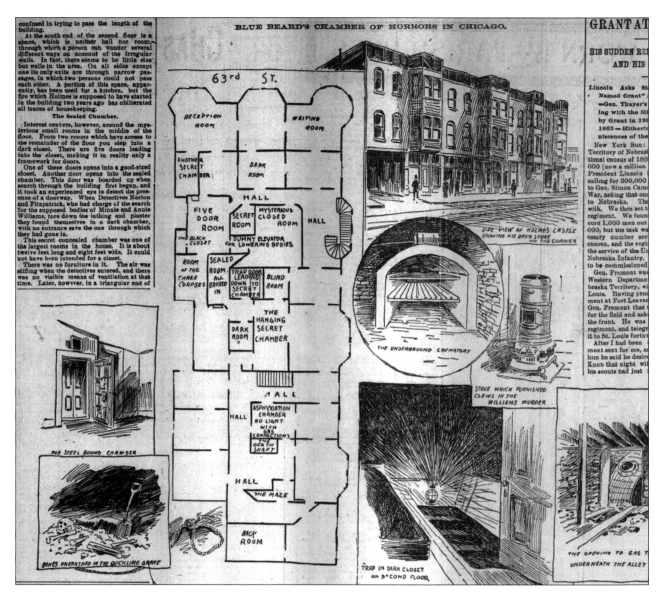

Newspaper illustration, published during the 1895 trial of Holmes, that shows the layout of his Chicago hotel, which was dubbed the "Murder Castle."

After the close of the World's Columbian Exposition in October 1893, business at the World's Fair Hotel declined sharply. In addition, Holmes's many fraudulent dealings were beginning to catch up to him. So he skipped town.

Holmes spent time in Fort Worth, Texas, where he apparently intended to build another hotel on land he inherited from a wealthy former fiancée and her sister. Holmes had slain both women. But the Fort Worth plans fell through.

An insurance scam would ultimately lead to Holmes's downfall. Holmes and Benjamin Pitezel had conspired to fake

Pitezel's death and collect on his $10,000 life insurance policy. Holmes would stage an explosion, leaving at the scene a disfigured cadaver that authorities would assume was Pitezel. Holmes would collect the insurance money on behalf of Pitezel's wife, while Pitezel went into hiding.

Herman Mudgett

Holmes and Pitezel would reunite later and split the money.

In October 1894, Holmes carried out the plan in Philadelphia. But instead of using a cadaver, he killed Pitezel. After receiving the insurance payment, Holmes left Philadelphia with three of Pitezel's children. He directed Mrs. Pitezel—who believed her husband was still alive—to follow with her other two children.

Holmes's scheme unraveled because he failed to pay another man who had played a minor role in the conspiracy. That man informed police. Holmes was apprehended in Boston in November 1894. He was returned to Philadelphia to face trial for the killing of Pitezel. While he waited in jail, investigators uncovered evidence of other murders Holmes had committed. Many skele-

tons and bone fragments were found at the World's Fair Hotel, which the press dubbed the "Murder Castle." The bodies of the Pitezel children were also found. Holmes had killed 15-year-old Alice and 11-year-old Nellie in Toronto, Canada; their 8-year-old brother, Howard, met his end in Irvington, Indiana.

In late 1895, Holmes was tried and convicted in the killing of Benjamin Pitezel. He was sentenced to death.

After his trial, Holmes confessed to murdering more than 100 people. He later revised the figure to 27, providing details of the killings in a story he wrote for the *Philadelphia Inquirer*. Many contemporary historians believe that Holmes significantly undercounted his victims in the *Inquirer* confession. The actual number of victims will never be known. This much is certain, however: Herman Mudgett, aka Dr. H. H. Holmes, relished killing. "I was born with the devil in me," Holmes confessed before he was hanged in 1896. "I could not help the fact that I was a murderer, no more than the poet can help the inspiration to sing."

DENNIS RADER
THE BTK KILLER

For 17 years, beginning in 1974, a serial murderer terrorized Wichita, Kansas. He killed people inside their own homes, detailing his exploits in communications with the local media and even proposing a nickname for himself: BTK. The letters stood for "Bind, Torture, Kill." That was what the murderer liked to do to his victims.

In 1991 the BTK murders mysteriously stopped, and there were no more communications from the killer. As the years passed, investigators and Wichita residents were left to wonder: Had the BTK killer died? Was he serving time in prison for another crime? Had he been incapacitated by a serious medical condition such as a stroke? Or had he simply moved out of the area and continued murdering somewhere else? As it turned out, none of these scenarios explained the inactivity of Wichita's serial killer. Dennis Rader, the BTK murderer, had

apparently done something once thought impossible for a serial killer: he had stifled his compulsion to kill.

Born in 1945, Rader grew up in Wichita. According to childhood friends and acquaintances, there seemed to be nothing unusual about the boy or his working-class family. Rader would later admit, however, that as a child he had tortured animals and developed a fetish for women's underwear.

After graduating from high school, Rader served a four-year stint in the U.S. Air Force. Following his discharge in 1970, he returned to Kansas. He married, bought a house in the Wichita suburb of Park City, and started a family. His wife gave birth to a son in 1975, and to a daughter three years later.

While working for a security company, Rader attended Kansas State University. In 1979 he received a bachelor's degree in criminal justice. He advanced in his job, receiving a promotion to supervisor. In his role overseeing the installation of alarm systems, Rader was consistently described as extremely organized and meticulous. But his insistence that everyone he supervised follow to the letter every company rule, and his stern reprimands for minor lapses, caused resentment.

Outside of work, Rader found time to get involved in the community. He became a Boy Scout leader. Other adults in his troop would remember him as demanding—he would never allow any of the boys to receive a badge unless they had completely mastered the relevant skill—but not unfair. Rader also served as an usher at, and eventually as congregation president of, the Christ Lutheran Church near Park City. The Raders unfailingly attended Sunday services there. Fellow worshipers would say that Rader treated his wife with the utmost respect and even doted on her.

But behind the façade of responsible worker, upstanding member of the community, and dedicated husband and family man lurked a sadistic killer. Rader committed his first murders on January 15, 1974. He went to the home of a former coworker, Julie Otero, cut the phone line, and waited by the back door. When someone opened the door to let out the family dog, Rader forced his way inside. Brandishing a pistol, he tied up Julie Otero; her husband,

CASE FILE

Name: Dennis Lynn Rader
Moniker: BTK
Born: March 9, 1945
Period of homicides: 1974–1991
Number of victims: 10
Captured: Feb. 25, 2005
Outcome of case: pled guilty to 10 counts of murder; sentenced to 10 consecutive life terms

Joseph; and their two children, 11-year-old Josephine and 9-year-old Joseph II. He suffocated or strangled them all with cords and plastic bags. According to his later testimony, Rader killed the male members of the Otero household only because he realized they could identify him. His intended victim was either Julie or Josephine. Rader obtained sexual gratification by tying up, slowly suffocating, and finally strangling women.

After the Otero murders, Rader soon moved on to another "project," as he called potential victims. While driving one day, he spotted 21-year-old Kathryn Bright entering her house. He stalked her for a while, learning as much as he could about her schedule and habits and planning her murder. On April 4, 1974, while Bright was out,

The body of one of the Otero family members is removed from 803 N. Edgemoor, the scene of the 1974 quadruple homicide committed by the BTK Killer.

Rader broke into her house and waited. He assumed Bright would be alone when she returned home, but her 19-year-old brother, Kevin, was with her. Though Rader succeeded in tying up the siblings at gunpoint, Kevin Bright broke free of his bonds and grappled with the older man. Rader shot him in the head and face, but Kevin Bright managed to stagger out the door. Rader stabbed Kathryn Bright to death and quickly fled. Wichita police initially didn't connect the Otero and Bright cases.

In October 1974, Rader left a letter in a public library. It included details about the Otero crime scene that only the killer could know. "I can't stop it so the monster goes on," the letter said, introducing the moniker "BTK" and promising more victims. Wichita police decided not to alert the public about the existence of the letter, fearing that doing so might compromise the Otero investigation.

Rader struck twice in 1977. He killed Shirley Vian Relford, a married woman with three young children, in March. In December he murdered Nancy Fox, a 25-year-old secretary. Rader actually called 911 to report the Fox slaying, in the process leaving a recording of his voice.

Rader clearly sought publicity, and his success in eluding capture fed his ego. In January 1978 he sent a communication about the Vian Relford murder to a local newspaper, the *Wichita Eagle*. Printed with a child's rubber-stamp set, it was in the form of a nursery rhyme. When the newspaper failed to report the communication, Rader sent a letter to television station KAKE. "How many do I have to kill," he complained, "before I get my name in the paper or get some national attention?"

In response to the letter, the Wichita Police Department finally went public with the information that a serial killer calling himself BTK was at large in the community. Despite the resulting deluge of newspaper and TV stories, Rader wasn't satisfied. He stalked a woman whose home was just a few blocks away from that of Nancy Fox. Rader broke into the woman's home one night in April 1979. She was spared a violent death only because she stayed late at a dance. A few months afterward, the woman received a package containing some items taken from her home, along with a poem and a drawing depicting what BTK had planned to do to her. A

similar package was dropped off at KAKE-TV.

In August 1979, the Wichita Police Department released an enhanced recording of the 911 call announcing the killing of Nancy Fox. The audio clip was broadcast dozens of times by local radio and TV stations. Unfortunately, no one identified BTK's voice as belonging to Dennis Rader.

The next BTK murder, in April 1985, demonstrated Rader's sense of invulnerability. The victim, 53-year-old Marine Hedge, lived on the same Park City block as Rader and his family. After strangling her in her home, Rader dumped her body several miles away.

Vicki Wegerle was the ninth BTK victim. In September 1986, Rader strangled the 28-year-old mother, but only after she had put up a ferocious fight. His difficulty controlling Wegerle was perhaps the reason Rader chose an older woman as his next victim. He killed Dolores Davis, a 62-year-old grandmother, in January 1991. It would be the last of the BTK slayings. Rader later confessed to finding gratification in the memories of his murders.

He also landed a new job that satisfied his need for power over the lives of other people. A few months after the Davis murder, Rader was hired as a Park City compliance officer. He was responsible for enforcing code regulations about keeping dogs on leash,

Some victims of the BTK Killer. From left: Vicki Wegerle, Dolores Davis, Marine Hedge, Nancy Fox, Shirley Vian Relford, and Kathryn Bright.

maintaining lawns, and the like. By all accounts, he delighted in issuing citations. Many residents complained about his petty and rude behavior, and two women filed harassment complaints against him.

Meanwhile, the Wichita community's terror over the BTK strangler subsided. Although police never stopped hunting for the killer, as the case grew cold, the large task force that had been set up was disbanded. A single detective, Lieutenant Kenneth Landwehr, stayed on the BTK case full time.

Then, in January 2004, the *Wichita Eagle* published a story to mark the 30th anniversary of the first BTK killings. A local lawyer was also writing a book about the case. Apparently this awakened Rader's massive ego: he wanted all the acclaim he believed his crimes merited. He also thought he was the only person who could tell the real story. In March 2004, Rader sent a letter, along with photos of Vicki Wegerle's body and a photocopy of her driver's

license, to the *Eagle*. A media frenzy ensued.

Over the next 11 months, at least 10 other communications from the killer—letters, packages, postcards, and more—were dropped off at TV stations or left in public places. One package included an outline of a book the killer proposed to write, called "The BTK Story." Another contained a word-search puzzle purportedly giving clues to BTK's crimes and identity. To throw off the police, Rader incorporated false information about his background into some of his communications.

Wichita police recognized the need to share information with the public, which might be able to help identify the killer. Profilers at the FBI's Behavioral Analysis Unit suggested a strategy that would encourage BTK to continue communicating but not provoke him to resume his murders. All media briefings were carefully scripted to avoid providing details about the direction of the investigation, or to inadvertently challenge or insult BTK. In addition, all briefings were conducted solely by Landwehr. This, the profilers hoped, would cause the killer to believe he had a rapport with the police detective.

The strategy paid off in early 2005. In January Rader left a message for the police that read: "Can I communicate with Floppy and not be traced to computer. Be honest." The note was signed "Rex." The police were directed to answer in the classified section of the *Eagle*. The notice they ran said, "Rex, it will be OK."

In February a local TV station received a package from BTK that included a computer disk. A police forensic specialist quickly recovered metadata indicating that the disk was opened on a computer belonging to the Christ Lutheran Church, and the document it contained was modified by a user named Dennis. The evidence strongly pointed to Christ Lutheran's congregation president, Dennis Rader, as the BTK strangler. To make sure, the Wichita district attorney issued a secret subpoena for the medical records of Rader's daughter. A comparison of her DNA with DNA obtained from the Otero crime scene showed that BTK was her father. On February 25, 2005, police arrested Dennis Rader.

Some writers would speculate that Rader had been captured only because he'd wanted to be caught. Nonsense,

Dennis Rader is escorted into a Kansas prison after his 2005 conviction.

responded former FBI profiler Gregg McCrary. "If he wanted to get caught," McCrary said, "he would have hung out at the crime scene. He just thought he was smarter than everybody else." Indeed, Rader expressed disbelief and anger upon learning that Wichita police had lied about being unable to track him through a computer disk.

In June 2005, Rader pled guilty to 10 counts of murder. He was later sentenced to 10 consecutive life terms.

GARY RIDGWAY
THE GREEN RIVER KILLER

Dave Reichert would never forget when the enormity of the situation first hit him. It was the afternoon of August 15, 1982, and Reichert—a homicide detective with the sheriff's department of King County, Washington—had been dispatched to the Seattle suburb of Kent. There, a rafter on a leisurely Sunday trip down the Green River had spotted the bodies of two young women just below the surface of the water. The bodies had been weighed down with rocks.

Reichert had never worked a serial murder case. But that's what this appeared to be. Just three days earlier, the body of another young woman had been found floating in the same vicinity of the Green River; four weeks before that, the corpse of a 16-year-old girl had been pulled from the river near Kent.

Reichert inched down the riverbank toward the submerged bodies of the latest victims. High grass and underbrush covered the ground. Reichert looked carefully for any small pieces of evidence the killer might inadvertently have left when he dragged the bodies to the river—a footprint, a bit of torn clothing, something that slipped out of a pocket. Instead the detective found another body. Blue pants were tied tightly around the young woman's neck.

Reichert suspected that the five victims thus far discovered represented only the beginning. He was right. Still, he could scarcely have imagined the scope of the horror that would unfold in the coming months and years. The unknown offender police dubbed the Green River Killer would dump dozens of bodies across Washington's King County—perhaps attaining the repugnant distinction of most prolific serial killer in U.S. history—before he was finally caught in 2001.

The Green River Killer began life in Salt Lake City, Utah, in 1949. Gary Ridgway was the middle of three sons of Thomas Ridgway, a bus driver, and his wife, Mary. The family moved frequently before settling in a working-class community south of Seattle in 1960.

By his own account, Gary Ridgway had a close but conflicted relationship with his mother, whom relatives have described as domineering. Both of his parents were strict disciplinarians.

Ridgway never did well in school. In fact, he wouldn't graduate from high school until after his 20th birthday. Still, classmates recalled him as well adjusted and rather ordinary. That assessment couldn't have been further from the truth. Ridgway was completely lacking in empathy, as a senseless crime he perpetrated at the age of 14 demonstrated. One day, while walking near his home, Ridgway encountered a six-year-old boy in a cowboy suit. He convinced the boy, who was playing alone, to accompany him into some nearby woods. There Ridgway plunged a knife into the little boy's side. For a while, he stood above his prone victim, grinning. Then he bent down and wiped the blade of his knife on the boy's shirt. "I always wanted to know what it felt like to kill somebody," Ridgway said as he strolled off, laughing heartily. Though the boy suffered a punctured liver and lost a great deal of blood, doctors managed to save his life.

CASE FILE

Name: Gary Leon Ridgway
Moniker: the Green River Killer
Born: Feb. 18, 1949
Period of known homicides: 1982–1998
Number of victims: at least 49; estimated at 71–90
Captured: Nov. 30, 2001
Outcome of case: pleaded guilty to 49 counts of first-degree murder; sentenced to life in prison without parole

Police never made an arrest in the case. Only decades later would Ridgway admit that he'd been the attacker.

In August 1969, shortly after graduating from high school, Ridgway enlisted in the U.S. Navy. The following summer he married a high school girlfriend, and the couple moved to San Diego. Ridgway soon shipped out on a six-month tour of duty in the Far East. While he was away, his 19-year-old wife had an extramarital affair. Ridgway was furious at this infidelity—notwithstanding the fact that during his deployment he'd begun a lifelong habit of patronizing prostitutes. He filed for divorce in September 1971, five weeks after being discharged from the navy.

Back in the Seattle area, Ridgway returned to a job he'd held briefly while in high school: as a painter at the Kenworth Truck Company. He would remain with Kenworth for three decades. While he earned a reputation as a model employee, hardworking and meticulous, some female coworkers would say his excessive attentions made them uncomfortable.

In 1973 Ridgway married for the second time. Two years later, his wife gave birth to a son. Outwardly, Ridgway appeared to be a deeply pious man. A regular churchgoer who joined two congregations, he was frequently moved to tears by Sunday sermons, according to his wife. At work he read the Bible during lunch breaks. He would often try to engage strangers on the topic of religion, and he was particularly animated when discussing the evils of prostitution. Secretly, however, Ridgway visited prostitutes on a routine basis.

By the late 1970s Ridgway's second marriage was disintegrating. His wife became increasingly alarmed by his behavior. He enjoyed sneaking up on her and scaring her, she said. On one occasion he choked her from behind for no apparent reason. In July 1980 Ridgway's wife left him, obtained a restraining order, and filed for divorce. She was awarded primary custody of their son, with Ridgway granted visitation rights every other weekend.

The body of the Green River Killer's first victim, 16-year-old Wendy Coffield, was found near the Meeker Street bridge in July 1982.

In mid-1981 Ridgway moved in with a new girlfriend in Seattle. By year's end she had asked him to leave, however, and Ridgway bought his own house in southern King County. The house, located in the small community of Des Moines, was just a few blocks from the Pacific Highway South. A nearby section of the highway, known locally as the SeaTac Strip, was notorious for prostitution. Ridgway would pick up many of his victims along the Strip. He murdered dozens of them in his house.

According to experts on serial homicide, an emotional stressor often precipitates the killer's first murder (though subsequent murders typically occur in the absence of such a trigger). Common stressors include serious conflict in, or the breakup of, a relationship; loss of a job; financial problems; and legal problems. In April 1982, financial problems forced Ridgway to rent his house and move into the garage (his tenants would remain for six months). In May, Ridgway was arrested for soliciting sex from an undercover sheriff's deputy disguised as a prostitute. The degree to which these difficulties contributed to his descent into murder is impossible to ascertain. His first victim, a 16-year-old who occasionally dabbled in prostitution, disappeared from her foster home in early July. What is clear, however, is that once he'd committed the first murder, Ridgway killed at an astonishing

A number of Ridgway's victims were last seen at this motel on the SeaTac Strip.

rate. By the end of 1982, he had claimed more than a dozen victims. He killed at least 24 more in 1983.

Ridgway's known victims ranged in age from 15 to 38, but the overwhelming majority were in their teens or early twenties. Occasionally he killed a young runaway or a hitchhiker, but almost all of his victims were prostitutes. Ridgway would speak of his deep hatred for women who sold their bodies, but he admitted that wasn't the only reason for his choice of victims. He believed that his victims, who were marginalized by society and often led transient lives, wouldn't be missed as much as other women. "I picked prostitutes," Ridgway said, "because I thought I could kill as many of them as I wanted without getting caught."

Police, however, were determined to catch the Green River Killer. On August 16, 1982—the day after Dave Reichert stumbled across a body on the banks of the river—King County officials announced the formation of a 25-member task force to work the case.

The announcement generated considerable publicity, and stories about the case would be splashed across the front pages of local newspapers as additional victims were discovered. A King County police captain called a press conference one year after the killings started. "Do not get into cars with anyone you don't know," he warned women. It would have been difficult to find a prostitute in the Seattle area who hadn't heard of the Green River Killer. Yet Ridgway still managed to find new victims. Like other serial killers the FBI designates as organized, Ridgway thought a lot about how best to commit his crimes, including how to put potential victims at ease. He went to great lengths to project a docile image. He sometimes gave rides to prostitutes along the SeaTac Strip without requesting their services. Later, when he did offer to pay for sex, they would tend to trust him. Often he would speak, with

conspicuous affection and pride, about his young son. He would show a wary prostitute a photo of the boy before she got into his truck. If he took her back to his house, he would make sure she saw the boy's bedroom, which was filled with toys. On at least one occasion, Ridgway even brought his son with him when he picked up a prostitute. They drove to an isolated area, and Ridgway told the boy to wait in the truck while he and the woman went into the woods. When Ridgway returned alone, the seven-year-old asked his father where the woman had gone. Ridgway said she'd decided to walk home.

After having sex with a victim, Ridgway strangled her from behind, either manually or with a ligature. He disposed of bodies in secluded areas, often in clusters, which he liked to revisit frequently. In addition to the Green River, these clusters would be found near Star Lake, the Seattle-Tacoma International Airport, the Snoqualmie River, and a pair of state highways. Ridgway also dumped several victims, or body parts of victims, near Tigard, Oregon.

Ridgway first drew police scrutiny in connection with the Green River case in 1983. On the evening of April 30, a man named Bobby Woods saw his 18-year-old girlfriend, Marie Malvar, get into a pickup truck in a motel parking lot along the SeaTac Strip. The dark-

Carol Estes holds a photo of her 15-year-old daughter Debra, who in September 1982 became the Green River Killer's ninth victim. The body of Debra Estes was not discovered until 1988.

colored vehicle had a distinctive patch of primer paint near the right front wheel. It appeared that Malvar and the driver were arguing as the truck pulled away, and Woods tried unsuccessfully to follow in his own car. After a couple days passed and he hadn't heard anything from Malvar, Woods told her father what he'd witnessed. The two of them, joined by Malvar's brother, searched the area for the dark pickup with the primer patch. They finally spotted it parked in front of a house in Des

Moines and called local police. A Des Moines police detective went to the residence. He spoke with the homeowner, Gary Ridgway, who claimed never to have met Malvar. After walking through the house and finding nothing out of the ordinary, the detective left.

The small police department of Des Moines treated Malvar's disappearance as a routine missing-persons case. A brief report was written and filed. No one recognized a possible connection with the Green River case.

Dave Reichert was a leading member of the Green River task force. He spent years trying to find the killer.

In retrospect, it's not difficult to understand why. Several months earlier, the Green River task force had quietly disbanded because investigators believed they'd identified the killer. A flawed psychological profile from the FBI had led the task force to focus on a taxi driver. The cabbie, an ex-convict, agreed to submit to a lie-detector test. When he denied knowing any of the Green River victims, the polygraph indicated that he was lying. Though police didn't have enough evidence to make an

arrest, they were keeping the suspect under constant surveillance.

Yet prostitutes continued to disappear from the Seattle area. In November 1983, Dave Reichert—who was supervising a handful of King County cops still working the Green River case—sent a detective to interview Gary Ridgway in connection with a missing prostitute. Vice squad officers had detained, but not arrested, Ridgway in the company of the woman about six weeks before she was last seen. Ridgway didn't arouse the King County detective's suspicions during the November 1983 interview. Undoubtedly the detective would have questioned Ridgway much more aggressively had he known about Marie Malvar's disappearance.

In January 1984 the Green River task force was reconstituted with 43 full-time officers, including Reichert. Before long, Ridgway had emerged as a "person of interest" in the investigation. One prostitute came forward to report that Ridgway had seemed intensely interested in what she knew about a victim of the Green River Killer. Another claimed that Ridgway had tried to strangle her in the woods, but she'd managed to escape after a struggle. Investigators called Ridgway in for questioning. He admitted that he sometimes paid for sex. But he disputed the account of the prostitute who said he'd tried to strangle her—he insisted that she'd actually attacked him—and he denied any involvement in the Green River murders. In mid-1984, Ridgway agreed to undergo a polygraph examination. He passed. The task force moved on; it had thousands of other names to investigate.

By early 1986 investigators had homed in on a fur trapper as the prime suspect. The man was known to trap in areas where the Green River Killer had dumped clusters of victims. He also had a history of sadistic behavior. A search of the trapper's home attracted extensive media coverage, but ultimately turned up no evidence linking him to the slayings. Within three months, the task force had officially cleared the man.

Ridgway's name again came to the fore with the unearthing of the long-overlooked Marie Malvar file. In April 1987 a judge issued a search warrant, and investigators scoured Ridgway's home and truck. They found nothing that conclusively linked the suspect to the Green River murders. The search warrant also authorized investigators to collect from Ridgway hair and saliva samples. These would be used for DNA "fingerprinting," a forensic technique that was then in its infancy. To the disappointment of investigators, Ridgway's DNA profile couldn't definitively be matched to semen found on some early victims of the Green River Killer. The investigation had apparently hit another dead end.

At this point, task force investigators believed that the Green River Killer had ceased murdering three years earlier. That wasn't correct, though Ridgway did dramatically slow down the pace of his killing, with only four confirmed victims after 1985. The explanation, Ridgway would later say, was that he'd begun dating a woman he genuinely loved. They married in 1988.

As the years passed with no apparent activity from the killer, the Green River task force was wound down. By 1991 only one detective, Tom Jensen, remained on the case. It seemed that the Green River Killer might never be caught.

That prospect haunted Dave Reichert, who thought he'd failed the families of the killer's many victims. "You are their hope," he said. "They rely on you to find out what happened to their daughters."

In 1997 Reichert was appointed sheriff of King County. He kept in close touch with Jensen about the status of the Green River investigation. Eventually, Reichert brought together 30 detectives who had served on the task force, asking them to think about new avenues that might be pursued to solve the case. In early 2001 Jensen, who'd been monitoring advances in DNA profiling, decided to have the biological evidence in the case reexamined. This time, using a newly developed

(Top) Investigators search for the remains of one of Ridgway's victims in 2003, after the killer agreed to tell police where bodies could be found in order to avoid the death penalty. (Bottom) Ridgway leaves a King County courtroom in December 2003 after receiving 48 life sentences without the possibility of parole. In February 2011, after another of his victims' bodies was found, a 49th life term was added to his sentence.

technology, a forensic scientist at Washington's state crime lab was able to conclude with certainty that Ridgway's saliva sample and semen samples taken from the bodies of Green River victims had come from the same person.

On November 30, 2001, Ridgway was arrested and charged with four counts of aggravated first-degree murder. At an initial hearing, he entered a plea of not guilty.

Meanwhile, Reichert had put together a team of investigators to connect Ridgway with other Green River murders. In March 2003, Ridgway was charged with three additional homicides after investigators matched microscopic paint particles on the victims' clothing with paint used at his workplace. He again pleaded not guilty.

Ridgway soon decided to accept a plea deal, however. He agreed to cooperate in the ongoing investigation, providing details of his killings and helping locate victims' remains, then to plead guilty to all the homicides with which he was charged. In exchange, prosecutors agreed not to pursue the death penalty.

On November 5, 2003, Ridgway pleaded guilty to 48 counts of aggravated first-degree murder. He was sentenced to life imprisonment without

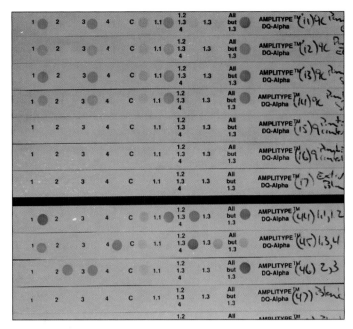

DNA testing eventually linked Ridgway to four of the Green River victims.

parole. Eight years later, after the body of another victim had been found, Ridgway was charged with and pleaded guilty to a 49th homicide.

But even that probably doesn't represent a full reckoning of Ridgway's murderous career. He confessed to killing more than 70 women, though there is insufficient evidence for further charges, in large part because Ridgway claims not to know the names or even remember the faces of victims. "I killed so many women," he said, "I have a hard time keeping them straight."

HAROLD SHIPMAN
DEADLY DOCTOR

The first telephone call took Angela Woodruff by surprise. The caller, an officer with the Greater Manchester police, informed Woodruff that her mother, Kathleen Grundy, had been found dead in her home. The death certificate—issued by her personal physician, Dr. Harold Shipman—listed the cause of death as old age. Though 81 years old, Mrs. Grundy had seemed the picture of health. The former mayor of Hyde, she'd remained very active in town affairs. She loved gardening, continued to do her own housework, and enjoyed regular five-mile walks. Woodruff had seen no signs that her mother's health was declining. So the call from police had been a shock.

The second telephone call, however, raised Angela Woodruff's suspicions. The caller, a solicitor (lawyer), informed Woodruff that his law firm was in possession of her mother's last will and tes-tament. It had arrived through the mail on June 24, 1998—the very day Mrs. Grundy had died. The will left the deceased's entire estate, worth more than £385,000, to Dr. Shipman.

Woodruff, who was also a solicitor, had previously handled all of her mother's legal affairs. This included drafting Mrs. Grundy's will, in 1986. It seemed odd that a dozen years later, her mother would prepare a new will, by herself and without so much as mentioning it to her daughter. It seemed odder still that she would leave nothing to Woodruff, her only child, or to her grandchildren, with whom she was very close.

Angela Woodruff decided to investigate the new will. The first thing she noticed about the document was how sloppily it had been typed. That didn't seem right, because her mother had been trained as a secretary and was always meticulous about her correspondence. Furthermore, while the will listed Mrs. Grundy's residence in Hyde, it included no reference to another property she owned. The signature seemed halting and much larger than usual for Mrs. Grundy. And when Woodruff tracked down the two people who had supposedly witnessed the will, they said they knew nothing about the document.

In late July 1998, Woodruff took her findings to the police. The ensuing investigation would unravel the sinister career of Dr. Harold Shipman, who is considered the most prolific serial killer in the history of England—and perhaps the entire world.

Harold Frederick Shipman was born in Nottingham, England, on January 14, 1946. Freddy, as he was called, was the second of three children of truck driver Harold Shipman and his wife, Vera. Though hers was a decidedly working-class family, Vera didn't view her Nottingham neighbors as social equals, according to people who knew the Shipman family. "Vera was friendly enough," a neighbor of the Shipmans would recall. "But she really did see her family as superior to the rest of us. Not only that, you could tell Freddy was her favorite, the one she saw as the most promising of her three children."

Young Freddy became the vessel for his mother's aspirations. She was highly controlling of her son's life, even determining which children were good

CASE FILE

Name: Harold Frederick Shipman

Moniker: Dr. Death

Born: Jan. 14, 1946

Period of homicides: 1975–1998

Number of victims: estimated at 250 or more (215 confirmed by official inquiry)

Captured: Sept. 7, 1998

Outcome of case: convicted of 15 counts of murder; sentenced to 15 consecutive life terms + 4 years

Died: January 13, 2004 (suicide)

enough to be his friends. Freddy grew up haughty, acquaintances remembered, and had an unusually close relationship with his mother.

Freddy was devastated when his beloved mother was diagnosed with lung cancer. As she wasted away from the effects of the disease, he remained her constant companion. Vera Shipman's final weeks were filled with excruciating pain. Her only relief came when the doctor arrived to administer a morphine injection. She succumbed to cancer, aged 43, in June 1963. Freddy was 17.

In 1965, two years after his mother's death, Shipman enrolled in medical school at the University of Leeds. He was aloof around classmates but did marry and start a family. Shipman graduated from medical school in 1970. He then went to work as a junior doctor at the Pontefract General Infirmary, a hospital in West Yorkshire.

In 1974 Shipman was accepted into a medical practice in Todmorden, another West Leeds town. Colleagues soon caught him writing phony prescriptions for the opioid painkiller pethidine. When confronted, Shipman claimed he was addicted to pethidine and pleaded for understanding. The senior doctors in the practice fired him instead.

Convicted of prescription fraud and forgery, Shipman received a fine but didn't lose his medical license, probably because he'd voluntarily entered a drug-rehab program. In 1977 he joined the staff of the Donneybrook Medical Centre, in Hyde, as a general practitioner. There he gained a reputation for his knowledge and hard work, though many colleagues also found him arrogant and abrasive. Shipman ultimately left Donneybrook, amid conflicts with fellow doctors, in 1993.

He established his own medical practice in Hyde, and it was soon thriving. Shipman seemed the epitome of an old-fashioned family doctor. He made

Harold Shipman

frequent house calls, especially for his many elderly patients, and was admired for his soothing bedside manner.

But not everyone thought highly of Shipman. By early 1998, a local undertaker named Alan Massey had grown suspicious of the doctor. Massey noticed how frequently he was called on to collect the body of one of Shipman's patients—invariably an elderly woman who lived alone—from the patient's home. He found an extraordinary number of these bodies fully clothed and reclining tranquilly on a chair or sofa. Why weren't there more bodies on the floor, as might be expected with a heart attack or stroke victim? Why weren't there more bodies in bed, as might be expected with someone who had suffered an extended illness? Massey suspected foul play. He shared his concerns with his daughter, also an undertaker, who sought the opinion of an area doctor. The doctor, noticing the unusual frequency with which Shipman signed cremation forms, brought the matter to the attention of the local coroner, who in turn contacted police.

The police investigation that followed would later be blasted as inept and perfunctory. Officers obtained a warrant for a secret search of the com-

View of Dr. Harold Shipman's medical clinic on Market Street in Hyde, which he operated from 1993 until his arrest in 1998.

puterized medical records of Shipman's deceased patients. The records consistently showed that Shipman had treated patients for the condition that he eventually certified as the cause of death. Satisfied that nothing was amiss, police detectives shut down their investigation. They'd failed to consider the possibility that Shipman had inserted false diagnoses and treatments into his patients' files after those patients were already dead.

But by July 1998, thanks to the tenacity of Angela Woodruff, another police investigation had been opened. Kathleen Grundy's body was exhumed, and tissue and hair samples were sent to a toxicologist. Meanwhile, police searched Shipman's home and office. They found a typewriter that, tests showed, had been used to type out the fake will. Shipman was arrested and charged with murder after the toxicologist's report revealed that Mrs. Grundy had died from a massive overdose of a morphine-like drug.

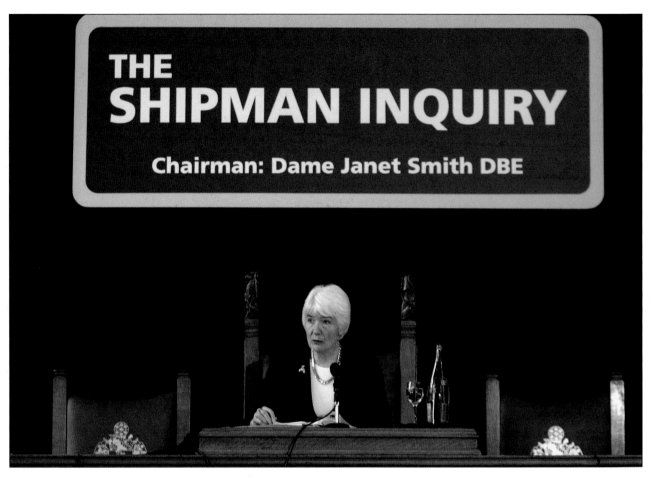

Although Shipman was convicted of 15 murders, an official government investigation determined that he had killed at least 215 people.

The police investigation quickly expanded to other possible victims. Additional bodies were exhumed.

Throughout, Shipman maintained his innocence. He mocked the detectives who questioned him for their supposed stupidity. "He was treating this as some sort of game," Detective Chief Inspector Mike Williams noted, "a competition, pitting . . . what he considered to be his superior intellect, to those of the officers who were interviewing him."

Shipman lost his smug attitude when police informed him that a computer forensic specialist had examined his files and found that, in case after case, backdated treatment notes had been inserted in the hours after the patient's death. Shipman, who fancied himself a computer expert, hadn't known that modifications to electronic files carry timestamps.

Police ultimately charged Shipman with murdering 15 women, including Kathleen Grundy, between 1995 and

1998. Shipman had paid a house call to each woman on the day of her death, and he had subsequently inserted back-dated entries into the patient's file. Some of the women had been cremated, but morphine toxicity was found to be the cause of death for those whose bodies could be exhumed and tested.

On January 31, 2000, after a four-month trial, Shipman was found guilty of murdering all of the women. The judge sentenced him to 15 consecutive life terms, plus four years for forging Kathleen Grundy's will.

Shipman would never be released from prison, but hardly anyone believed that he'd killed only 15 people. Professor Richard Baker of Leicester University did a statistical analysis of Shipman's entire medical career. In a report released in 2001, Baker concluded that the death rate among Shipman's patients was abnormally high, and specifically that 236 more of Shipman's patients had died in their homes than would be expected. Baker also found that Shipman had probably begun killing in the mid-1970s, during his time at Todmorden. The Shipman Inquiry—a blue-ribbon commission chaired by Dame Janet Smith, a respected British judge—reached similar conclusions.

Smith confirmed 215 victims, beginning in 1975 with 70-year-old Eva Lyons and ending in 1998 with Kathleen Grundy. In addition, there was solid if not conclusive evidence suggesting that Shipman had killed about three dozen others, bringing the probable death toll to 250 or more. Most of the victims were elderly women, but the list also included elderly men, a handful of middle-aged men and women, and even a four-year-old child. Only in the Grundy killing—by which Shipman stood to benefit financially—was there an obvious motive.

On January 14, 2004, Shipman hanged himself in his prison cell. His death, and the fact that he never confessed, left unanswered the question of why England's most prolific serial killer had injected so many people with lethal doses of morphine, pethidine, or similar drugs. Was he ritually reenacting the end of his mother's life? Was he angry that his victims had lived longer than his mother? Coroner John Pollard, who had worked with Shipman, offered a simpler explanation. "I think the only valid possible explanation . . . is that he simply enjoyed viewing the process of dying," Pollard said, "and enjoyed the feeling of control over life and death."

FRED WEST
THE MONSTER OF GLOUCESTER

"Fred has been here for 21 years," a neighbor of Fred West's told a newspaper reporter. "I've known him ever since he's been here. If you asked anybody in the street you couldn't wish for a better fellow. . . . He was a kind man. He thought the world of his kids."

That view, though shared widely by neighbors and acquaintances of Fred West, was completely wrong. West wasn't a good fellow, he wasn't kind, and he certainly didn't think the world of his kids. He was a sadistic serial rapist and murderer whose victims included his own children. But, like other psychopaths, West was able to conceal his depravity behind a mask of normalcy, and even a certain superficial charm.

Frederick Walter Stephen West, the son of English farmworkers, was born and raised in Much Marcle, a small rural village northwest of Gloucester.

He and his five siblings grew up in poverty. West would later accuse his father of incest and bestiality, but there is no evidence to substantiate those charges.

At age 15, West dropped out of school and went to work full time as a farm laborer. His life appeared unremarkable until 1958. In November of that year, he fractured his skull in a motorcycle accident, remaining in a coma for more than a week. After his recovery, family members noticed behavioral changes, including frequent displays of rage.

In the years that followed, West would be in and out of trouble with the law. Most of his arrests were for minor offenses, such as petty theft. But, at age 19, West was charged with rape after getting a 13-year-old family friend pregnant. He was convicted on the lesser charge of child molestation and received a fine instead of a jail sentence.

In 1962, at age 21, West married an old girlfriend named Catherine Costello. Theirs was a volatile relationship, and within a few years Costello had returned to her native Scotland, leaving West with a daughter, Rose, and a stepdaughter, Charmaine. West immediately took up with Costello's friend Anne McFall. She became pregnant and started demanding that West marry her. Instead, in the summer of 1967, he killed McFall and dismembered her body, which he buried in a field near Much Marcle. McFall is believed to be West's first murder victim.

Shortly after McFall's death, Costello returned from Scotland in an attempt to reconcile with her husband. She gave up after a few months, however.

West soon met and began a relationship with 15-year-old Rosemary Letts. She had grown up in a troubled household, with a mother who suffered from depression and a violent, schizophrenic father who may have had an incestuous relationship with his daughter. For West, Rosemary Letts proved to be an ideal partner. Though a bit slow intellectually, she was eager to assist him in whatever depraved act he sought to commit.

The couple moved to Gloucester, where in 1970 Letts gave birth to a daughter. Late that year, West received a prison sentence for theft. In June

CASE FILE

Name: Frederick Walter Stephen West
Born: Sept. 29, 1941
Period of homicides: 1967–1987
Number of victims: at least 11
Captured: Feb. 24, 1994
Outcome of case: charged with 12 murders; committed suicide before trial
Died: Jan. 1, 1995

1971, right before West was released, Letts killed Charmaine West because she wouldn't cry when beaten. Curious neighbors who noticed the child's absence were informed that Charmaine had gone to Scotland to live with her mother.

Catherine Costello actually did intend to take Charmaine with her to Scotland. But when she arrived in Gloucester to pick her daughter up, West murdered her. That killing took place in August 1971. Six months later, in January 1972, West and Rosemary Letts were married.

To accommodate their growing family, the couple moved into a roomy house at 25 Cromwell Street, Gloucester. Neighbors came to know them as decent and hardworking people. Fred West, a handyman, was always

Fred West involved his wife Rosemary in many murders.

ready to help with someone's home-improvement project—despite the fact that he always seemed to be working on his own house. The Wests' many children (Rosemary would eventually have seven) impressed neighbors as polite and well behaved.

But behind the walls of 25 Cromwell Street, in the basement that Fred West soundproofed, unspeakable acts were committed. West regularly raped his

daughters, occasionally filming the assaults. He and Rosemary sexually abused, tortured, and murdered young women they picked up hitchhiking, hired as nannies for their children, or took in as lodgers. West dismembered the victims' bodies—always taking fingers and toes as trophies—before burying them in a backyard garden, beneath the cellar and garage additions he constructed, or under the patio he built.

One of the victims buried under the patio was the Wests' oldest daughter, Heather. Fred West killed the 16-year-old in 1987, after learning that she had mentioned his assaults to a friend. The Wests claimed that Heather had gotten a job in another city. But their children sensed the truth. On occasion Fred West warned them not to join Heather under the patio, which was understood to be the consequence of sharing family secrets.

Nevertheless, in 1992 another daughter told schoolmates that her father had raped her. One of the girls shared the story with her mother, who contacted the Gloucester police. After an investigation, police arrested Fred West. He was charged with rape. Rosemary West was charged as an accomplice. But prosecutors eventually dropped the charges when two crucial witnesses refused to testify.

Detective Constable Hazel Savage wasn't satisfied, however. Savage had interviewed the West children in the course of the rape investigation. She considered their account of Heather's sudden departure from the household rather suspicious. Savage tried to locate Heather by searching national tax, insurance, and medical rolls. She found no records after 1987. Meanwhile, the detective learned from social workers that the West children had made what seemed like joking references to joining Heather under the patio. Savage feared that this represented more than just macabre humor.

On the afternoon of February 24, 1994, police served a search warrant and starting digging up the Wests' property. They unearthed the remains of Heather beneath the patio but unexpectedly found other remains as well. A weeks-long excavation of the backyard, cellar, and garage addition West had built yielded nine victims in total. West confessed to killing all nine, in addition to Charmaine Costello and Catherine West, whose bodies he'd disposed of elsewhere. Eventually police also found the remains of Anne McFall, and West

Police sift through soil in the garden at the Wests' former home in Gloucester, searching for the remains of their victims, during April 1994.

was charged with her murder as well. Investigators strongly suspected there were more victims, though they couldn't find enough evidence to bring further charges.

West insisted that he'd committed all the murders on his own, without the participation or even knowledge of his wife. But circumstantial evidence linked Rosemary West to many of the killings. Under intense police interrogation, she gave inconsistent and often contradictory accounts of various events. In April 1994, she was charged with 10 homicides.

Fred West would never answer for his crimes in court. On January 1, 1995, while awaiting trial on 12 counts of murder, he hanged himself in his prison cell.

In November 1995, a jury convicted Rosemary West of 10 homicides. She received a life sentence. Evidence introduced at the trial indicated that Fred West had been involved in all of the killings except that of his stepdaughter Charmaine.

Curiosity-seekers from across England began flocking to 25 Cromwell Street for a glimpse of the residence the press had dubbed "the House of Horrors." Many citizens of Gloucester found the spectacle repugnant. For them, the house stood as a constant reminder of the unspeakable evil that had been perpetrated in their midst. Seeking to help Gloucester turn the page on a terrible chapter in its history, the city council in October 1996 purchased the Wests' property and ordered the house demolished. A simple pathway now runs through the lot where nine girls and young women met violent ends.

AILEEN WUORNOS
VICTIM TURNED KILLER?

During the 1970s and 1980s, when the FBI's Behavioral Science Unit first undertook a systematic examination of serial murderers, profilers believed that only men engaged in serial killing. "Women do commit multiple murders, of course," noted the FBI profiler Robert Ressler, "but they tend to do so in a spree, and not sequentially." Aileen Wuornos would prove Ressler and his colleagues at the BSU wrong. Yet Wuornos's case would bear out another important finding of the BSU: that childhood neglect and abuse are often linked to serial murder later in life.

Abandoned by her teenaged mother before her fourth birthday, Wuornos was raised by her grandparents, including her alcoholic and physically abusive grandfather. She became pregnant at age 14, allegedly after being raped by a friend of her grandfather's. Wuornos put the baby up for adoption, but her grandfather threw her out of his house shortly afterward. Fifteen years old and homeless, she turned to prostitution to support herself.

In 1976 Wuornos drifted from her native Michigan to Florida. There, at age 20, she met and married a wealthy 69-year-old man. But she soon began beating her husband, who filed a restraining order against her. The marriage ended after less than two months.

In the years that followed, Wuornos—a heavy drinker and drug user—would be arrested for offenses ranging from assault and armed robbery to auto theft and forgery. She served a jail sentence in 1982–1983 for robbing a convenience store.

In 1986 Wuornos met Tyria Moore, a hotel maid, at a gay bar in Daytona. They became a couple, living together in a succession of trailers, cheap motels,

CASE FILE

Name: Aileen Carol Wuornos

Born: Feb. 29, 1956

Period of homicides: 1989–1990

Number of victims: 7

Captured: Jan. 9, 1991

Outcome of case: convicted of one murder, pled no contest or guilty to five other murders; sentenced to death

Died: Oct. 9, 2002 (executed by lethal injection)

and run-down apartments in central Florida.

For a while, Wuornos made enough money as a prostitute to support herself and Moore. But in November 1989, she began killing men and stealing their money and belongings. What caused this shift to murder? Wuornos would later insist that her first victim, a 51-year-old electronics-store owner named Richard Mallory, assaulted her after agreeing to pay for sex. She shot him to death in self-defense, Wuornos said. While that claim cannot be verified, it certainly is plausible: Mallory had previously served a prison term for sexual assault.

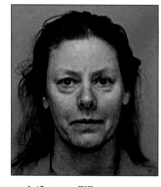

Aileen Wuornos

In any event, Wuornos actively sought more victims after killing Mallory. Her modus operandi was to hitchhike until a white, middle-aged man driving alone stopped and offered her a ride. She would propose to have sex with the man, but would instead pull a handgun from her purse and shoot him. In addition to Mallory, Wuornos eventually confessed to killing six men in this manner.

By the fall of 1990, authorities suspected that a serial killer was at work in central Florida. Six bodies of men killed with a small-caliber handgun had been discovered in remote or wooded areas in the region. Investigators searched pawnshops and eventually located items belonging to two of the victims. Thumbprints left when the items were pawned were matched to Aileen Wuornos. On January 9, 1991, she was arrested outside a biker bar in Port Orange.

Tyria Moore, who was promised immunity from prosecution, enticed Wuornos to confess in telephone conversations with her jailed lover. In January 1992, Wuornos was tried and convicted for the murder of Richard Mallory. The jury sentenced her to death.

Wuornos would receive five additional death sentences after pleading no contest or guilty to five

Cells on death row at Florida State Prison, where Aileen Wuornos was executed in 2002. The prison previously housed several other infamous serial killers, including Ted Bundy; Danny Rolling, who had murdered five girls; Gerard John Schaefer, a former police officer who may have killed more than 30 young women; and Ottis Toole, whose victims included Adam Walsh, a seven-year-old whose 1981 disappearance drew national attention.

other murders. She confessed to a seventh homicide, but the victim's body was never found, and prosecutors decided not to try her in that case.

For nearly a decade, lawyers for Wuornos appealed her death sentences. They argued that the courts had failed to adequately consider mitigating factors, including the history of abuse Wuornos had suffered and her supposedly diminished mental capacity. But Wuornos insisted that she'd known exactly what she was doing and didn't regret her murders. "I'm one who seriously hates human life and would kill again," she wrote in a letter to the Florida Supreme Court, requesting that her appeals be ended. Wuornos wanted to die, and on October 9, 2002, she got her wish. The state of Florida put the 46-year-old serial killer to death by lethal injection.

CHAPTER NOTES

p. 7:   "It's not just the gruesomeness . . ." Kate Stone Lombardi, "Author and Expert on Serial Killers Who Relishes His Work," *New York Times*, March 28, 1999. http://www.nytimes.com/1999/03/28/nyregion/author-and-expert-on-serial-killers-who-relishes-his-work.html

p. 12: "three or more separate events. . ." John Douglas et al., *Crime Classification Manual: A Standard System for Investigating and Classifying Violent Crimes*, 2nd ed. (San Francisco: Jossey-Bass, 2006), 96–97.

p. 16: "Now that I've got you . . ." Douglas Martin, "John Falotico, Detective Who Arrested Berkowitz, Dies at 82," *New York Times*, March 15, 2006. http://www.nytimes.com/2006/03/15/nyregion/15falotico.html?n=Top/Reference/Times%20Topics/People/B/Berkowitz,%20David?ref=davidberkowitz&pagewanted=print&_moc.semityn.www

p. 17: "The girls call me ugly . . ." Cited in Pat Brown, *Killing for Sport: Inside the Minds of Serial Killers* (Beverly Hills, CA: Phoenix Books, 2008), 80.

p. 18: "I AM . . ." Tom Philbin and Michael Philbin, *The Killer Book of Serial Killers: Incredible Stories, Facts and Trivia from the World of Serial Killers* (Napierville, IL: Sourcebooks, 2009), 124.

p. 19: "Sam's a thirsty lad . . ." Cited in Bryan Ethier, *True Crime: New York City—The City's Most Notorious Criminal Cases* (Mechanicsburg, PA: Stackpole Books, 2010), 47.

p. 23: "He admitted that . . ." Robert K. Ressler and Tom Shachtman, *Whoever Fights Monsters* (New York: St. Martin's Paperbacks, 1993), 77.

p. 24: "Everything I saw about him . . ." Cheryl McCall, "The Enigma of Ted Bundy: Did He Kill 18 Women? Or Has He Been Framed?" *People* vol. 13, no. 1 (January 7, 1980). http://www.people.com/people/archive/article/0,,20075542,00.html

p. 24: "I'm the most cold-blooded . . ." Robert D. Hare, *Without Conscience: The Disturbing World of the Psychopaths Among Us* (New York: The Guilford Press, 1999), 52.

p. 25: "I didn't know what made . . ." Stephen G. Michaud and Hugh Aynesworth, *The Only Living Witness: The True Story of Serial Sex Killer Ted Bundy* (Irving, TX: Authorlink Press, 1999), 66.

p. 28: "I liked Ted immediately . . ." Ibid., 86.

p. 31: "You always sensed . . ." Robert Gehrke, "A Wrong Turn Led to Ted Bundy's Twisted Road to Justice," *Los Angeles Times*, September 3, 2000. http://articles.latimes.com/2000/sep/03/local/me-14716

p. 35: "You feel the last bit . . ." Sebastian Junger, *A Death in Belmont* (New York: Harper Perennial, 2007), 78.

p. 42: "had lost his only . . ." Harold Schechter, *Deviant* (New York: Simon & Schuster, 1998), 31.

p. 48: "Dear Boss . . ."Facsimile, "Dear Boss" letter, Casebook: Jack the Ripper. http://www.casebook.org/ripper_letters/

p. 49: "The Juwes are . . ." History of the Metropolitan Police, "The Enduring Mystery of Jack the Ripper." http://www.met.police.uk/history/ripper.htm

p. 49: "I was not codding . . ." "The 'Saucy Jacky' Postcard," Casebook: Jack the Ripper. http://www.casebook.org/ripper_letters/

p. 50: "From hell . . ." "The 'From Hell' Letter," Ibid.

p. 57: "I was born with the devil . . ." H. H. Holmes, quoted in Erik Larson, *The Devil in the White City: Murder, Magic, and Madness at the Fair that Changed America* (New York: Vintage Books, 2004), 109.

p. 60: "I can't stop it . . ." Monica Davey, "Suspect in 10 Kansas Murders Lived an Intensely Ordinary Life," *New York Times*, March 6, 2005. http://www.nytimes.com/2005/03/06/national/06btk.html?pagewanted=1&_r=1

p. 61: "How many do I have to kill . . ." Jeff Chu, "Was the Killer Next Door?" *Time* (March 7, 2005). http://www.time.com/time/magazine/article/0,9171,1034731-1,00.html

p. 63: "Can I communicate with Floppy . . ." cited in Norman D. Williams and Kenneth Landwehr, "Bind, Torture, Kill: The BTK Investigation," *The Police Chief*, vol. 73, no. 12 (December 2006). http://www.policechiefmagazine.org/magazine/index.cfm?fuseaction=display_arch&article_id=1065&issue_id=122006

p. 63: "Rex, it will be OK," Ibid.

p. 63: "If he wanted to be caught . . ." Chu, "Was the Killer Next Door?"

p. 65: "I always wanted to know . . ." Sean Robinson, "What Made Ridgway Kill Still a Riddle," *News Tribune* (Tacoma), November 9, 2003. http://www.thenewstribune.com/2003/11/09/366408/what-made-ridgway-kill-still-a.html

p. 68: "I picked prostitutes . . ." Karen Hucks, "Gary Leon Ridgway's Confession: 'I Killed So Many,'" *News Tribune* (Tacoma), November 6, 2003. http://www.thenewstribune.com/2003/11/06/366432/gary-leon-ridgways-confession.html

p. 68: "Do not get into cars . . ." Tomas Guillen and Carlton Smith, "Police Net Catches the Wrong Man," *Seattle Times*, September 17, 1987. http://seattletimes.com/news/local/greenriver/1987/part4.html

p. 71: "You are their hope . . ." Terry McCarthy, "River of Death," *Time* (Feb. 27, 2003). http://www.time.com/time/magazine/article/0,9171,250023,00.html

p. 73: "I killed so many . . ." Hucks, "Ridgway's Confession."

p. 75: "Vera was friendly enough . . ." Nigel Cawthorne, *Serial Killers & Mass Murderers: Profiles of the World's Most Barbaric Killers* (Berkeley, CA: Ulysses Press, 2007), 272.

p. 78: "He was treating this . . ." Cited in "Profile of a Killer Doctor," *BBC News World Edition*, January 31, 2000. http://news.bbc.co.uk/2/hi/in_depth/uk/2000/the_shipman_murders/the_shipman_files/611013.stm

p. 79: "I think the only valid . . ." Ibid.

p. 80: "Fred has been here . . ." Will Bennett and Marianne Macdonald, "Inside 25 Cromwell Street: The 'Genial Neighbour' at No 2," *The Independent* (January 2, 1995). http://www.independent.co.uk/news/uk/inside-25-cromwell-street-the-genial-neighbour-at-no-25-1566338.html

p. 85: "Women do commit . . ." Ressler and Shachtman, *Whoever Fights Monsters*, 93.

p. 87: "I'm one who seriously . . ." Cited in Paul Pinkham, "Execution Due Tomorrow for Killer," *Florida Times-Union*, October 8, 2002. http://jacksonville.com/tu-online/stories/100802/met_10640647.shtml

GLOSSARY

disorganized—characteristic of or describing a type of serial killer who is of average or below average intelligence, who tends to be socially awkward and isolated, and whose murders involve less planning.

enuresis—the inability to control urination by a person who is old enough to be capable of such control.

ligature—a cord or other item used to tie or bind someone tightly.

lothario—a man whose chief interest is seducing women.

modus operandi—a distinct pattern or method of operation by which a criminal commits crimes.

organized—characteristic of or describing a type of serial killer who is of higher intelligence, is socially adept, and whose murders are carefully planned.

postmortem—done or performed after death.

psychopath—an individual exhibiting a set of antisocial personality traits and behaviors, including compulsive lying, failure to accept responsibility for personal actions, extreme narcissism, lack of empathy, impulsivity, and lack of guilt or remorse.

psychosis—a loss of contact with reality, as evidenced by hallucinations, delusions, or disordered speech or behavior.

schizophrenia—a serious, chronic brain disorder characterized by delusional thinking and behavior, often accompanied by auditory or visual hallucinations.

signature—in the context of serial murder, an action (such as postmortem mutilation of a body) that isn't necessary to perpetrate the crime but that the killer does ritually for emotional satisfaction.

FURTHER READING

Douglas, John, and Mark Olshaker. *Journey into Darkness*. New York: Simon & Schuster, 1997.

Fox, James A., Jack A. Levin, and Kenna Quinet. *The Will to Kill: Making Sense of Senseless Murder*. 4th ed. Needham Heights, MA: Allyn & Bacon, 2011.

Hare, Robert D. *Without Conscience: The Disturbing World of the Psychopaths Among Us*. New York: The Guildford Press, 1999.

Hickey, Eric. *Serial Murderers and Their Victims*. 5th ed. Belmont, CA: Wadsworth, 2010.

Holmes, Ronald M., and Stephen T. Holmes. *Serial Murder*. 3rd ed. Thousand Oaks, CA: SAGE Publications, 2010.

Larson, Erik. *The Devil in the White City: Murder, Magic, and Madness at the Fair that Changed America*. New York: Vintage Books, 2004.

McCrary, Gregg O., with Katherine Ramsland. *The Unknown Darkness: Profiling the Predators Among Us*. New York: HarperCollins, 2003.

Ressler, Robert, and Tom Shachtman. *I Have Lived in the Monster: Inside the Minds of the World's Most Notorious Serial Killers*. New York: St. Martin's, 1998.

Schechter, Harold, and David Everitt. *The A to Z Encyclopedia of Serial Killers*. 2nd ed. New York: Pocket Books, 2006.

INTERNET RESOURCES

http://www.fbi.gov/stats-services/publications/serial-murder

This monograph from the FBI, "Serial Murder: Multi-Disciplinary Perspectives for Investigators," presents an overview of serial murder as well as issues of concern for law enforcement and criminal justice professionals.

http://news.bbc.co.uk/2/hi/in_depth/uk/2000/the_shipman_murders/the_ship-man_files/611013.stm

An in-depth examination of the case of Dr. Harold Shipman, from the BBC.

http://www.casebook.org

This website is devoted to the Jack the Ripper case.

http://www.biography.com/people/groups/serial-killers

The website for the Biography television network includes biographies of 35 infamous serial killers, including Ted Bundy, Ed Gein, H.H. Holmes, and Aileen Wournos.

http://www.kansas.com/btk

The *Wichita Eagle*'s comprehensive coverage of the BTK Strangler case includes an in-depth profile of killer Dennis Rader, information on his victims, historic photos, court records, a timeline, and more.

http://www.murderuk.com/serial_killers.html

A database of serial killers in the UK.

INDEX

".44 Caliber Killer." *See* Berkowitz, David ("Son of Sam")

Albert Victor (Prince), 51–52
antisocial personality disorder (ASPD), 15
Arnold, Thomas, 48–49
arson, *17*
Aynesworth, Hugh, 34

Baker, Richard, 79
Báthory, Erzsébet, 8
behavioral profiling, *11*, 12, 38, 70
    See also serial killers
Berkowitz, David ("Son of Sam"), 16–17
    and arson, *17*
    capture of, 16, 21–22
    confession of, 22–23
    letters of, 18–19, *20*
    and media coverage, 19–20
    murders of, 16, 17, 18, 19, 21, 32–33
Berkowitz, Nathan, 16–17
Berkowitz, Pearl, 16
Bianchi, Kenneth, 37–38
    and multiple-personality disorder, 41
    murders of, 36, 37, 38–41
    as pimp, 38
    trial of, 41
Boone, Carole, 28, 32, 34
Bowman, Margaret, 33
Breslin, Jimmy, 19
Bright, Kathryn, 59–60, *62*
Bright, Kevin, 60
BTK Killer. *See* Rader, Dennis ("BTK Killer")
Bundy, Johnnie, 25
Bundy, Ted, 9–10, *87*

capture of, 30–31
charisma of, 24, 26, 28
childhood of, 24–25
escape of, from jail, 32
execution of, 35
investigation of, 30–32
murders of, 25, 27–30, 33, 34–35
in politics, 24, 25–27
trials of, 31, 32, 33–34
Buono, Angelo, Jr.
    marriages of, 36–37
    murders of, 36, 37, 38–40
    as pimp, 38
    trial of, 41

Campbell, Caryn, 30, 32
Carr, Sam, 22–23
"the Castle." *See* "World's Fair Hotel"
Chapman, Annie, 47–48
Chase, Richard Trenton, 14, *15*
Coffield, Wendy, *66*
Columbian Exposition (Chicago World's Fair), 53, 54–56
    See also "World's Fair Hotel"
Corona, Juan, 9
Costello, Catherine, 81, 83
Costello, Charmaine. *See* West, Charmaine
Cowell, Eleanor Louise, 24–25
Cowell, Theodore Robert. *See* Bundy, Ted
Crime Classification Manual, 12–13

DaRonch, Carol, 29–30, 31
Davis, Dolores, 61, *62*
Davis, Ross, 24, 26–27
"DC Snipers," *12*
DeBurger, James E., 14

Numbers in **bold italics** refer to captions.

DeSalvo, Albert (Boston Strangler), 9
"disorganized" serial killers, 11–12
    See also serial killers
Douglas, John, 10–11, 12
Druitt, Montague John, 51, *52*
    See also Jack the Ripper

Eddowes, Catherine, 48–49, 51
enuresis (bed-wetting), 11, 13
Estes, Carol, *69*
Estes, Debra, *69*
Evans, Daniel, 26, *27*

Falco, Richard David. See Berkowitz,
    David ("Son of Sam")
Falotico, John, 16, 22
Fisher, Michael, 31
Fletcher, Art, 25–26
Fox, Nancy, 61, *62*

Gacy, John Wayne, 9
Gein, Augusta, 42
Gein, Ed, 42–43
    murders of, 43
Gein, George, 42
Gein, Henry, 42
Gilles de Rais, 8
Green River Killer. See Ridgway, Gary
    ("Green River Killer")
Grundy, Kathleen, 74–75, 77, 78, 79
Gull, William, 52

Hagmeier, William, 34, 35
Hanson, Stewart, 31
Hayward, Bob, 30–31
Healy, Lynda Ann, 27
Hedge, Marine, 61, *62*
hedonistic serial killers, 14
    See also serial killers
Hillside Stranglers. See Bianchi, Kenneth;
    Buono, Angelo, Jr.
Hogan, Mary, 43
Holmes, H. H. See Mudgett, Herman ("H.
    H. Holmes")
Holmes, Ronald M., 13–14
Hudspeth, Cindy, 39–40

Jack the Ripper, 7
    letters from, 48, 49–50

and media coverage, 47, 50
    murders of, 45–51
    theories concerning, 51–52
Jensen, Tom, 71

Kelly, Mary, 51
Kent, Debra, 30
Keppel, Bob, 31, 34
Kloepfer, Elizabeth, 26, 27, 28–29, 30, 31
Krafft-Ebing, Richard von, 8–9

Landwehr, Kenneth, 62, 63
Leach, Kimberly Diane, 33
"Leather Apron," 46–47
    See also Jack the Ripper
Letts, Rosemary. See West, Rosemary
    (Mrs. Fred West)
Levy, Lisa, 33
Lombroso, Cesare, 8
Lupo, Sal, *21*
Lusk, George, 50
"lust killers," 9, 14
    See also serial killers
Lyons, Eva, 79

Macdonald triad, 11, 13
    See also serial killers
Mallory, Richard, 86
Malvar, Marie, 68–69, 70, 71
Malvo, Lee Boyd, *12*
Mandic, Karen, 40, 41
Martinez, Bob, 35
"mass murders," 9
    See also serial killers
Massey, Alan, 75
McCrary, Gregg, 63
McFall, Anne, 81, 83
Michaud, Stephen, 25, 34
mission-oriented serial killers, 14
    See also serial killers
Moore, Tyria, 85–86
Moscowitz, Stacy, 21
Mudgett, Herman ("H. H. Holmes"), 7,
    53–54
    insurance scam of, 56–57
    murders of, 54, 55, 56, 57
    and the World's Fair Hotel, 53, 54–56,
        57
Muhammad, John Allen, *12*

Mullin, Herbert, 14–15

Naslund, Denise, 29
Netley, John, 52
Nichols, Mary Ann ("Polly"), 46–47

Operation Omega, 18–19, 20–22
    See also Berkowitz, David ("Son of
        Sam")
"organized" serial killers, 11
    See also serial killers
Otero, Joseph, 59
Otero, Joseph II, 59
Otero, Josephine, 59
Otero, Julie, 59
Ott, Janice, 29

paranoid schizophrenia, 14, 23
personality disorders, 15
Pitezel, Alice, 57
Pitezel, Benjamin, 55, 56–57
Pitezel, Howard, 57
Pitezel, Nellie, 57
Placido, Judy, 21
Pollard, John, 79
power/control-oriented serial killers, 14
    See also serial killers
profiling, 11, 12, 38, 70
    See also serial killers
Psycho (movie), 42
psychopathy, 15

Rader, Dennis ("BTK Killer"), 58–59, 61–62
    letters from, 60, 61, 62–63
    murders of, 59–61
Ramirez, Richard ("Night Stalker"), 10
Reichert, Dave, 34, 64, 68, 70, 71, 73
Ressler, Robert K., 9, 10–11, 12, 13, 23,
    34, 85
Ridgway, Gary ("Green River Killer"), 34
    investigation of, 68–71, 73
    marriages of, 65, 66, 71
    murders of, 64, 65, 67–68, 73
    and prostitutes, 65, 66, 67–68, 70–71
    trial of, 72, 73
Ridgway, Mary, 65
Ridgway, Thomas, 65
Roberts, John, 11
Rolling, Danny, 87

Saldivar, Efren, 13
Salisbury (Lord), 52
Savage, Hazel, 82–83
Schaefer, Gerard John, 87
Schechter, Harold, 7
serial killers
    abuse of, as children, 11, 13, 85
    and behavioral profiling, 11, 12, 38, 70
    categorization of, 11–12, 13–14
    characteristics of, 10–11
    definition of, 9, 12–13
    and frequency of crimes, 7
    gender of, 11, 13, 85
    and gender of victims, 15
    in history, 7–8
    and insanity, 14–15, 23
    and "lust killers," 9, 14
    and the Macdonald triad, 11, 13
    as mythic figures, 7
    scientific study of, 8–9, 10–14
    and supernatural forces, 8
    as a team, 36, 38–39, 81
Sherman, Lydia, 8
Shipman, Harold, 13, 74–75
    death of, 79
    investigation of, 76–78
    medical practice of, 74, 75–77
    murders of, 75, 77–79
Shipman, Vera, 75
Shipman Inquiry, 79
    See also Shipman, Harold
Sickert, Walter, 52
The Silence of the Lambs (movie), 42
Smith, Janet, 79
"Son of Sam." See Berkowitz, David ("Son
    of Sam")
Stride, Elizabeth, 48, 49
Stumpp, Peter, 8

Tauria, Donna, 18
Thompson, Jerry, 31
Toole, Ottis, 87

Valenti, Jody, 18
Vian Relford, Shirley, 60–61, 62
Violante, Robert, 21
visionary serial killers, 14
    See also serial killers
Voskerichian, Virginia, 18, 19

Walsh, Adam, **87**
Warren, Charles, 48–49
Washington, Yolanda, 38
Weckler, Kristina, 38, 40
Wegerle, Vicki, 61, 62
West, Charmaine, 81, 83, 84
West, Fred, 80
    death of, 84
    investigation of, 82–84
    marriages of, 81, 82–83
    motorcycle accident of, 80
    murders of, 81, 82, 83–84
    as rapist, 80–81, 82
West, Heather, 82, 83
West, Rose, 81
West, Rosemary (Mrs. Fred West), 81–82, 84
"Whitechapel Murders," 45–51
    See also Jack the Ripper

Williams, Mike, 78
Williams, Wayne, 10
Woodruff, Angela, 74–75, 77
Woods, Bobby, 68–69
Worden, Bernice, 43
"World's Fair Hotel," 53, 54–56, 57
    See also Mudgett, Herman ("H. H. Holmes")
Wuornos, Aileen, 13
    death of, 87
    marriage of, 85
    murders of, 86–87

Yocom, David, 31

Zigo, Ed, 21–22

About the Author: Seth H. Pulditor, a freelance writer based in New York, is the author of several books for young adults, including *Fascism* (Mason Crest, 2013). A graduate of St. Joseph's University in Philadelphia, his interests include history, politics, and music.